The Essential

AIR FRYER

Cookbook for Beginners UK

2000+ Days Easy, Budget-Friendly & Tasty Recipes Book with Tips & Tricks for Air Frying, Grilling, and Baking - Ready In Less Than 30 Minutes

Petra Cechova

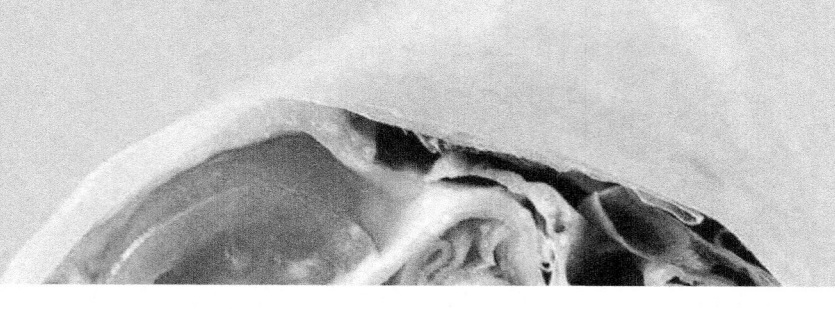

Copyright© 2024 By Petra Cechova

All rights reserved worldwide.

No part of this book may be reproduced or transmitted in any form or by any means, electronic or mechanical, including photo- copying, recording or by any information storage and retrieval system, without written permission from the publisher, except for the inclusion of brief quotations in a review.

Warning-Disclaimer

The purpose of this book is to educate and entertain. The author or publisher does not guarantee that anyone following the techniques, suggestions, tips, ideas, or strategies will become successful. The author and publisher shall have neither liability or responsibility to anyone with respect to any loss or damage caused, or alleged to be caused, directly or indirectly by the information contained in this book.

TABLE OF CONTENTS

1		Introduction
3	Chapter 1	Breakfasts
13	Chapter 2	Family Favorites
15	Chapter 3	Fast and Easy Everyday Favourites
19	Chapter 4	Snacks and Starters
26	Chapter 5	Poultry
35	Chapter 6	Beef, Pork, and Lamb
44	Chapter 7	Fish and Seafood
52	Chapter 8	Vegetables and Sides
59	Chapter 9	Vegetarian Mains
63	Chapter 10	Desserts
66	Appendix 1:	Basic Kitchen Conversions & Equivalents
67	Appendix 2:	Recipes Index

INTRODUCTION

Welcome to "The Essential Air Fryer Cookbook for Beginners UK." This cookbook is your key to unlocking the potential of the air fryer, an appliance that has revolutionized the way we cook by offering a healthier, faster, and more convenient method to prepare delicious meals. Designed with UK culinary traditions in mind, this book aims to guide you through the basics and beyond, ensuring you get the most out of your air fryer.

◆ Air frying is a game-changer in the kitchen. It promises the crispy, satisfying textures of fried foods but with significantly less oil, making it a healthier choice. The air fryer works by circulating hot air around the food, creating a crispy layer on the outside while keeping the inside tender and juicy. This makes it perfect for a wide range of dishes, from classic British staples to modern, inventive recipes.

◆ As a professional recipe writer, I have dedicated myself to exploring the capabilities of the air fryer. This book is the culmination of extensive testing and refinement, designed to provide you with recipes that are not only easy to follow but also highlight the unique advantages of air frying. Whether you're a complete beginner or looking to expand your repertoire, you'll find recipes here that suit your needs and inspire your creativity.

◆ The recipes in this cookbook celebrate the rich and diverse culinary heritage of the UK. From traditional fish and chips to modern favorites, every dish has been crafted to work perfectly in the air fryer. Imagine biting into a piece of fish that's golden and crispy, without the excessive oil of deep frying. Or enjoying perfectly roasted vegetables that are tender and caramelized, making for a delicious and nutritious side dish.

◆ One of the standout features of the air fryer is its versatility. It's not just for frying; it can bake, roast, and even grill. This means you can prepare a full English breakfast with crispy bacon and perfectly cooked sausages, bake a batch of scones, or roast a Sunday joint, all with one appliance. The recipes in this book reflect this versatility, offering you a variety of meals to enjoy any time of the day.

◆ Breakfasts become a breeze with the air fryer. From crispy hash browns to fluffy scrambled eggs, you can create a range of breakfast favorites with minimal effort and cleanup. Lunches and dinners are equally easy, with recipes for succulent chicken breasts, juicy burgers, and flavorful vegetarian dishes. The air fryer ensures that your meals are cooked evenly and quickly, saving you time while still delivering great taste.

◆ Vegetable lovers will rejoice at how the air fryer brings out the best in fresh produce. The hot air circulation caramelizes the natural sugars in vegetables, enhancing their flavors and giving them a delightful texture. Whether it's sweet potato fries, roasted Brussels sprouts, or a medley of seasonal vegetables, the air fryer makes it simple to create healthy and delicious sides.

◆ Meat and seafood dishes are elevated to new heights with the air fryer. It locks in juices while creating a crisp exterior, perfect for dishes like crispy chicken wings, juicy steaks, and tender fish fillets. Each recipe is designed to make the most of these qualities, ensuring your meals are both satisfying and healthy.

◆ Even baking is within your reach with the air fryer. You can whip up batches of cookies, muffins, and other baked goods that are golden brown and deliciously tender. The air fryer's precise temperature control makes it a reliable tool for all your baking needs.

◆ This cookbook is not just about recipes; it's also about providing you with the knowledge and confidence to use your air fryer to its fullest. You'll find tips on how to preheat your air fryer, arrange food for even cooking, and adjust cooking times and temperatures. These practical insights will help you achieve perfect results every time.

◆ In addition to its culinary benefits, the air fryer is also a convenient appliance for busy lifestyles. It heats up quickly, cooks food faster than conventional ovens, and is easy to clean. This means you can enjoy homemade meals without spending hours in the kitchen, making it a great tool for anyone looking to eat healthier without sacrificing convenience.

◆ "The Essential Air Fryer Cookbook for Beginners UK" is more than just a collection of recipes; it's a guide to a healthier, more efficient way of cooking. It's about embracing a tool that makes it easier to prepare and enjoy delicious meals, whether you're cooking for yourself, your family, or friends. This book aims to inspire you to try new recipes, experiment with different ingredients, and most importantly, enjoy the process of cooking.

◆ So, get ready to embark on a culinary journey with your air fryer. With this book, you'll discover how easy it is to create a wide range of dishes that are both healthy and delicious. From the first crispy bite to the last savory morsel, your air fryer will become your favorite kitchen companion. Welcome to the world of air frying, where every meal is a step towards healthier, tastier, and more enjoyable cooking.

Chapter 1

Breakfasts

Chapter 1 Breakfasts

Bacon and Spinach Egg Muffins

Prep time: 7 minutes | Cook time: 12 to 14 minutes | Serves 6

- 6 large eggs
- 60 ml double (whipping) cream
- ½ teaspoon sea salt
- ¼ teaspoon freshly ground black pepper
- ¼ teaspoon cayenne pepper (optional)
- 180 g frozen chopped spinach, thawed and drained
- 4 strips cooked bacon, crumbled
- 60 g grated Cheddar cheese

1. In a large bowl (with a spout if you have one), whisk together the eggs, double cream, salt, black pepper, and cayenne pepper (if using). 2. Divide the spinach and bacon among 6 silicone muffin cups. Place the muffin cups in your air fryer basket. 3. Divide the egg mixture among the muffin cups. Top with the cheese. 4. Set the air fryer to 150°C. Bake for 12 to 14 minutes, until the eggs are set and cooked through.

Bacon, Broccoli and Cheese Bread Pudding

Prep time: 30 minutes | Cook time: 48 minutes | Serves 2 to 4

- 230 g streaky bacon, cut into ¼-inch pieces
- 700 g brioche bread or rolls, cut into ½-inch cubes
- 3 eggs
- 235 ml milk
- ½ teaspoon salt
- freshly ground black pepper
- 235 g frozen broccoli florets, thawed and chopped
- 350 g grated Emmental cheese

1. Preheat the air fryer to 200°C. 2. Air fry the bacon for 6 to 10 minutes until crispy, shaking the basket a few times while it cooks to help it cook evenly. Remove the bacon and set it aside on a paper towel. 3. Air fry the brioche bread cubes for 2 minutes to dry and toast lightly. (If your brioche is a few days old and slightly stale, you tin omit this step.) 4. Butter a cake pan. Combine all the ingredients in a large bowl and toss well. Transfer the mixture to the buttered cake pan, cover with aluminium foil and refrigerate the bread pudding overnight, or for at least 8 hours. 5. Remove the casserole from the refrigerator an hour before you plan to cook, and let it sit on the countertop to come to room temperature. 6. Preheat the air fryer to 170°C. Transfer the covered cake pan, to the basket of the air fryer, lowering the dish into the basket using a sling made of aluminium foil (fold a piece of aluminium foil into a strip about 2-inches wide by 24-inches long). Fold the ends of the aluminium foil over the top of the dish before returning the basket to the air fryer. Air fry for 20 minutes. Remove the foil and air fry for an additional 20 minutes. If the top starts to brown a little too much before the custard has set, simply return the foil to the pan. The bread pudding has cooked through when a skewer inserted into the center comes out clean.

Strawberry Toast

Prep time: 10 minutes | Cook time: 8 minutes | Makes 4 toasts

- 4 slices bread, ½-inch thick
- Butter-flavoured cooking spray
- 235 g sliced strawberries
- 1 teaspoon sugar

1. Spray one side of each bread slice with butter-flavoured cooking spray. Lay slices sprayed side down. 2. Divide the strawberries among the bread slices. 3. Sprinkle evenly with the sugar and place in the air fryer basket in a single layer. 4. Air fry at 200°C for 8 minutes. The bottom should look brown and crisp and the top should look glazed.

Egg in a Hole

Prep time: 5 minutes | Cook time: 5 minutes | Serves 1

- 1 slice bread
- 1 teaspoon butter, softened
- 1 egg
- Salt and pepper, to taste
- 1 tablespoon grated Cheddar cheese
- 2 teaspoons diced gammon

1. Preheat the air fryer to 170°C. Place a baking dish in the air fryer basket. 2. On a flat work surface, cut a hole in the center of the bread slice with a 2½-inch-diameter biscuit cutter. 3. Spread the butter evenly on each side of the bread slice and transfer to the baking dish. 4. Crack the egg into the hole and season as desired with salt and pepper. Scatter the grated cheese and diced gammon on top. 5. Bake in the preheated air fryer for 5 minutes until the bread is lightly browned and the egg is cooked to your preference. 6. Remove from the basket and serve hot.

Bacon Eggs on the Go

Prep time: 5 minutes | Cook time: 15 minutes | Serves 1

- 2 eggs
- 110 g bacon, cooked
- Salt and ground black pepper, to taste

1. Preheat the air fryer to 200ºC. Put liners in a regular cupcake tin. 2. Crack an egg into each of the cups and add the bacon. Season with some pepper and salt. 3. Bake in the preheated air fryer for 15 minutes, or until the eggs are set. Serve warm.

Banana-Nut Muffins

Prep time: 5 minutes | Cook time: 15 minutes | Makes 10 muffins

- Oil, for spraying
- 2 very ripe bananas
- 95 g packed light soft brown sugar
- 80 ml rapeseed oil or vegetable oil
- 1 large egg
- 1 teaspoon vanilla extract
- 90 g plain flour
- 1 teaspoon baking powder
- 1 teaspoon ground cinnamon
- 120 g chopped walnuts

1. Preheat the air fryer to 160ºC. Spray 10 silicone muffin cups lightly with oil. 2. In a medium bowl, mash the bananas. Add the soft brown sugar, rapeseed oil, egg, and vanilla and stir to combine. 3. Fold in the flour, baking powder, and cinnamon until just combined. 4. Add the walnuts and fold a few times to distribute throughout the batter. 5. Divide the batter equally among the prepared muffin cups and place them in the basket. You may need to work in batches, depending on the size of your air fryer. 6. Cook for 15 minutes, or until golden brown and a toothpick inserted into the center of a muffin comes out clean. The air fryer tends to brown muffins more than the oven, so don't be alarmed if they are darker than you're used to. They will still taste great. 7. Let cool on a wire rack before serving.

Bunless Breakfast Turkey Burgers

Prep time: 5 minutes | Cook time: 15 minutes | Serves 4

- 450 g turkey banger meat, removed from casings
- ½ teaspoon salt
- ¼ teaspoon ground black pepper
- 60 g seeded and chopped green pepper
- 2 tablespoons mayonnaise
- 1 medium avocado, peeled, pitted, and sliced

1. In a large bowl, mix banger meat with salt, black pepper, pepper, and mayonnaise. Form meat into four patties. 2. Place patties into ungreased air fryer basket. Adjust the temperature to 190ºC and air fry for 15 minutes, turning patties halfway through cooking. Burgers will be done when dark brown and they have an internal temperature of at least 74ºC. 3. Serve burgers topped with avocado slices on four medium plates.

Garlicky Knots with Parsley

Prep time: 10 minutes | Cook time: 10 minutes | Makes 8 knots

- 1 teaspoon dried parsley
- 60 ml melted butter
- 2 teaspoons garlic powder
- 1 (312 g) tube refrigerated French bread dough, cut into 8 slices

1. Preheat the air fryer to 180ºC 2.Combine the parsley, butter, and garlic powder in a bowl 3.Stir to mix well 4.Place the French bread dough slices on a clean work surface, then roll each slice into a 6-inch-long rope 5.Tie the ropes into knots and arrange them on a plate 6.Brush the knots with butter mixture 7.Transfer the knots into the air fryer 8.You need to work in batches to avoid overcrowding 9.Air fry for 5 minutes or until the knots are golden brown 10.Flip the knots halfway through the cooking time 11.Serve immediately.

Bacon-and-Eggs Avocado

Prep time: 5 minutes | Cook time: 17 minutes | Serves 1

- 1 large egg
- 1 avocado, halved, peeled, and pitted
- 2 slices bacon
- Fresh parsley, for serving (optional)
- Sea salt flakes, for garnish (optional)

1. Spray the air fryer basket with avocado oil. Preheat the air fryer to 160ºC. Fill a small bowl with cool water. 2. Soft-boil the egg: Place the egg in the air fryer basket. Air fry for 6 minutes for a soft yolk or 7 minutes for a cooked yolk. Transfer the egg to the bowl of cool water and let sit for 2 minutes. Peel and set aside. 3. Use a spoon to carve out extra space in the center of the avocado halves until the cavities are big enough to fit the soft-boiled egg. Place the soft-boiled egg in the center of one half of the avocado and replace the other half of the avocado on top, so the avocado appears whole on the outside. 4. Starting at one end of the avocado, wrap the bacon around the avocado to completely cover it. Use cocktail sticks to hold the bacon in place. 5. Place the bacon-wrapped avocado in the air fryer basket and air fry for 5 minutes. Flip the avocado over and air fry for another 5 minutes, or until the bacon is cooked to your liking. Serve on a bed of fresh parsley, if desired, and sprinkle with salt flakes, if desired. 6. Best served fresh. Store extras in an airtight container in the fridge for up to 4 days. Reheat in a preheated 160ºC air fryer for 4 minutes, or until heated through.

Vanilla Muesli

Prep time: 5 minutes | Cook time: 40 minutes | Serves 4

- 235 g porridge oats
- 3 tablespoons maple syrup
- 1 tablespoon sunflower oil
- 1 tablespoon coconut sugar
- ¼ teaspoon vanilla
- ¼ teaspoon cinnamon
- ¼ teaspoon sea salt

1. Preheat the air fryer to 120ºC. 2. Mix together the oats, maple syrup, sunflower oil, coconut sugar, vanilla, cinnamon, and sea salt in a medium bowl and stir to combine. Transfer the mixture to a baking pan. 3. Place the pan in the air fryer basket and bake for 40 minutes, or until the muesli is mostly dry and lightly browned. Stir the muesli four times during cooking. 4. Let the muesli stand for 5 to 10 minutes before serving.

Hearty Cheddar Biscuits

Prep time: 10 minutes | Cook time: 22 minutes | Makes 8 biscuits

- 250 g self-raising flour
- 2 tablespoons sugar
- 120 g butter, frozen for 15 minutes
- 120 g grated Cheddar cheese, plus more to melt on top
- 315 ml buttermilk
- 235 g plain flour, for shaping
- 1 tablespoon butter, melted

1. Line a buttered 7-inch metal cake pan with parchment paper or a silicone liner. 2. Combine the flour and sugar in a large mixing bowl. Grate the butter into the flour. Add the grated cheese and stir to coat the cheese and butter with flour. Then add the buttermilk and stir just until you tin no longer see streaks of flour. The dough should be quite wet. 3. Spread the plain (not self-raising) flour out on a small baking sheet. With a spoon, scoop 8 evenly sized balls of dough into the flour, making sure they don't touch each other. With floured hands, coat each dough ball with flour and toss them gently from hand to hand to shake off any excess flour. Put each floured dough ball into the prepared pan, right up next to the other. This will help the biscuits rise, rather than spreading out. 4. Preheat the air fryer to 190ºC. 5. Transfer the cake pan to the basket of the air fryer. Let the ends of the aluminium foil sling hang across the cake pan before returning the basket to the air fryer. 6. Air fry for 20 minutes. Check the biscuits twice to make sure they are not getting too brown on top. If they are, re-arrange the aluminium foil strips to cover any brown parts. After 20 minutes, check the biscuits by inserting a toothpick into the center of the biscuits. It should come out clean. If it needs a little more time, continue to air fry for two extra minutes. Brush the tops of the biscuits with some melted butter and sprinkle a little more grated cheese on top if desired. Pop the basket back into the air fryer for another 2 minutes. 7. Remove the cake pan from the air fryer. Let the biscuits cool for just a minute or two and then turn them out onto a plate and pull apart. Serve immediately.

Simple Scotch Eggs

Prep time: 5 minutes | Cook time: 25 minutes | Serves 4

- 4 large hard boiled eggs
- 1 (340 g) package pork banger meat
- 8 slices streaky bacon
- 4 wooden cocktail sticks, soaked in water for at least 30 minutes

1. Slice the banger meat into four parts and place each part into a large circle. 2. Put an egg into each circle and wrap it in the banger. Put in the refrigerator for 1 hour. 3. Preheat the air fryer to 230ºC. 4. Make a cross with two pieces of streaky bacon. Put a wrapped egg in the center, fold the bacon over top of the egg, and secure with a toothpick. 5. Air fry in the preheated air fryer for 25 minutes. 6. Serve immediately.

Honey-Apricot Muesli with Greek Yoghurt

Prep time: 10 minutes | Cook time: 30 minutes | Serves 6

- 235 g porridge oats
- 60 g dried apricots, diced
- 60 g almond slivers
- 60 g walnuts, chopped
- 60 g pumpkin seeds
- 60 to 80 ml honey, plus more for drizzling
- 1 tablespoon rapeseed oil
- 1 teaspoon ground cinnamon
- ¼ teaspoon ground nutmeg
- ¼ teaspoon salt
- 2 tablespoons sugar-free dark chocolate crisps (optional)
- 700 ml fat-free natural yoghurt

1. Preheat the air fryer to 130ºC. Line the air fryer basket with parchment paper. 2. In a large bowl, combine the oats, apricots, almonds, walnuts, pumpkin seeds, honey, rapeseed oil, cinnamon, nutmeg, and salt, mixing so that the honey, oil, and spices are well distributed. 3. Pour the mixture onto the parchment paper and spread it into an even layer. 4. Bake for 10 minutes, then shake or stir and spread back out into an even layer. Continue baking for 10 minutes more, then repeat the process of shaking or stirring the mixture. Bake for an additional 10 minutes before removing from the air fryer. 5. Allow the muesli to cool completely before stirring in the chocolate crisps (if using) and pouring into an airtight container for storage. 6. For each serving, top 120 ml Greek yoghurt with 80 ml muesli and a drizzle of honey, if needed.

Chapter 1 Breakfasts

Everything Bagels

Prep time: 15 minutes | Cook time: 14 minutes | Makes 6 bagels

- 415 g grated Cheddar cheese or goat cheese Mozzarella
- 2 tablespoons unsalted butter or coconut oil
- 1 large egg, beaten
- 1 tablespoon apple cider vinegar
- 120 g blanched almond flour
- 1 tablespoon baking powder
- ⅛ teaspoon fine sea salt
- 1½ teaspoons sesame seeds or za'atar

1. Make the dough: Put the Mozzarella and butter in a large microwave-safe bowl and microwave for 1 to 2 minutes, until the cheese is entirely melted. Stir well. Add the egg and vinegar. Using a hand mixer on medium, combine well. Add the almond flour, baking powder, and salt and, using the mixer, combine well. 2. Lay a piece of parchment paper on the countertop and place the dough on it. Knead it for about 3 minutes. The dough should be a little sticky but pliable. (If the dough is too sticky, chill it in the refrigerator for an hour or overnight.) 3. Preheat the air fryer to 180ºC. Spray a baking sheet or pie dish that will fit into your air fryer with avocado oil. 4. Divide the dough into 6 equal portions. Roll 1 portion into a log that is 6 inches long and about ½ inch thick. Form the log into a circle and seal the edges together, making a bagel shape. Repeat with the remaining portions of dough, making 6 bagels. 5. Place the bagels on the greased baking sheet. Spray the bagels with avocado oil and top with everything bagel seasoning, pressing the seasoning into the dough with your hands. 6. Place the bagels in the air fryer and bake for 14 minutes, or until cooked through and golden brown, flipping after 6 minutes. 7. Remove the bagels from the air fryer and allow them to cool slightly before slicing them in half and serving. Store leftovers in an airtight container in the fridge for up to 4 days or in the freezer for up to a month.

Breakfast Calzone

Prep time: 15 minutes | Cook time: 15 minutes | Serves 4

- 350 g grated Cheddar cheese
- 60 g blanched finely ground almond flour
- 30 g full-fat soft cheese
- 1 large whole egg
- 4 large eggs, scrambled
- 230 g cooked banger meat, removed from casings and crumbled
- 8 tablespoons grated mild Cheddar cheese

1. In a large microwave-safe bowl, add Mozzarella, almond flour, and soft cheese. Microwave for 1 minute. Stir until the mixture is smooth and forms a ball. Add the egg and stir until dough forms. 2. Place dough between two sheets of parchment and roll out to ¼-inch thickness. Cut the dough into four rectangles. 3. Mix scrambled eggs and cooked banger together in a large bowl. Divide the mixture evenly among each piece of dough, placing it on the lower half of the rectangle. Sprinkle each with 2 tablespoons Cheddar. 4. Fold over the rectangle to cover the egg and meat mixture. Pinch, roll, or use a wet fork to close the edges completely. 5. Cut a piece of parchment to fit your air fryer basket and place the calzones onto the parchment. Place parchment into the air fryer basket. 6. Adjust the temperature to 190ºC and air fry for 15 minutes. 7. Flip the calzones halfway through the cooking time. When done, calzones should be golden in color. Serve immediately.

Scotch Eggs

Prep time: 10 minutes | Cook time: 20 to 25 minutes | Serves 4

- 2 tablespoons flour, plus extra for coating
- 450 g banger meat
- 4 hard-boiled eggs, peeled
- 1 raw egg
- 1 tablespoon water
- Oil for misting or cooking spray
- Crumb Coating:
- 90 g breadcrumbs
- 90 g flour

1. Combine flour with banger meat and mix thoroughly. 2. Divide into 4 equal portions and mould each around a hard-boiled egg so the banger completely covers the egg. 3. In a small bowl, beat together the raw egg and water. 4. Dip banger-covered eggs in the remaining flour, then the egg mixture, then roll in the crumb coating. 5. Air fry at 180ºC for 10 minutes. Spray eggs, turn, and spray other side. 6. Continue cooking for another 10 to 15 minutes or until banger is well done.

Cheddar-Ham-Corn Muffins

Prep time: 10 minutes | Cook time: 6 to 8 minutes per batch | Makes 8 muffins

- 90 g cornmeal/polenta
- 30 g flour
- 1½ teaspoons baking powder
- ¼ teaspoon salt
- 1 egg, beaten
- 2 tablespoons rapeseed oil
- 120 ml milk
- 120 g grated mature Cheddar cheese
- 120 g diced gammon
- 8 foil muffin cups, liners removed and sprayed with cooking spray

1. Preheat the air fryer to 200ºC. 2. In a medium bowl, stir together the cornmeal, flour, baking powder, and salt. 3. Add egg, oil, and milk to dry ingredients and mix well. 4. Stir in grated cheese and diced gammon. 5. Divide batter among the muffin cups. 6. Place 4 filled muffin cups in air fryer basket and bake for 5 minutes. 7. Reduce temperature to 170ºC and bake for 1 to 2 minutes or until toothpick inserted in center of muffin comes out clean. 8. Repeat steps 6 and 7 to cook remaining muffins.

Egg Tarts

Prep time: 10 minutes | Cook time: 17 to 20 minutes | Makes 2 tarts

- ⅓ sheet frozen puff pastry, thawed
- Cooking oil spray
- 120 g grated Cheddar cheese
- 2 eggs
- ¼ teaspoon salt, divided
- 1 teaspoon minced fresh parsley (optional)

1. Insert the crisper plate into the basket and the basket into the unit. Preheat the unit by selecting BAKE, setting the temperature to 200ºC, and setting the time to 3 minutes. Select START/STOP to begin. 2. Lay the puff pastry sheet on a piece of parchment paper and cut it in half. 3. Once the unit is preheated, spray the crisper plate with cooking oil. Transfer the 2 squares of pastry to the basket, keeping them on the parchment paper. 4. Select BAKE, set the temperature to 200ºC, and set the time to 20 minutes. Select START/STOP to begin. 5. After 10 minutes, use a metal spoon to press down the center of each pastry square to make a well. Divide the cheese equally between the baked pastries. Carefully crack an egg on top of the cheese, and sprinkle each with the salt. Resume cooking for 7 to 10 minutes. 6. When the cooking is complete, the eggs will be cooked through. Sprinkle each with parsley (if using) and serve.

Banger Stuffed Peppers

Prep time: 15 minutes | Cook time: 15 minutes | Serves 4

- 230 g spicy pork banger meat, removed from casings
- 4 large eggs
- 110 g full-fat soft cheese, softened
- 60 g tinned diced tomatoes, drained
- 4 green peppers
- 8 tablespoons grated chilli cheese
- 120 ml full-fat sour cream

1. In a medium frying pan over medium heat, crumble and brown the banger meat until no pink remains. Remove banger and drain the fat from the pan. Crack eggs into the pan, scramble, and cook until no longer runny. 2. Place cooked banger in a large bowl and fold in soft cheese. Mix in diced tomatoes. Gently fold in eggs. 3. Cut a 4-inch to 5-inch slit in the top of each pepper, removing the seeds and white membrane with a small knife. Separate the filling into four servings and spoon carefully into each pepper. Top each with 2 tablespoons cheese. 4. Place each pepper into the air fryer basket. 5. Adjust the temperature to 180ºC and set the timer for 15 minutes. 6. Peppers will be soft and cheese will be browned when ready. Serve immediately with sour cream on top.

Cinnamon Rolls

Prep time: 10 minutes | Cook time: 20 minutes | Makes 12 rolls

- 600 g grated Cheddar cheese
- 60 g soft cheese, softened
- 120 g blanched finely ground almond flour
- ½ teaspoon vanilla extract
- 96 ml icing sugar-style sweetener
- 1 tablespoon ground cinnamon

1. In a large microwave-safe bowl, combine Cheddar cheese, soft cheese, and flour. Microwave the mixture on high 90 seconds until cheese is melted. 2. Add vanilla extract and sweetener, and mix 2 minutes until a dough forms. 3. Once the dough is cool enough to work with your hands, about 2 minutes, spread it out into a 12 × 4-inch rectangle on ungreased parchment paper. Evenly sprinkle dough with cinnamon. 4. Starting at the long side of the dough, roll lengthwise to form a log. Slice the log into twelve even pieces. 5. Divide rolls between two ungreased round nonstick baking dishes. Place one dish into air fryer basket. Adjust the temperature to 190ºC and bake for 10 minutes. 6. Cinnamon rolls will be done when golden around the edges and mostly firm. Repeat with second dish. Allow rolls to cool in dishes 10 minutes before serving.

Maple Muesli

Prep time: 5 minutes | Cook time: 40 minutes | Makes 475 ml

- 235 g porridge oats
- 3 tablespoons pure maple syrup
- 1 tablespoon sugar
- 1 tablespoon neutral-flavoured oil, such as refined coconut or sunflower
- ¼ teaspoon sea salt
- ¼ teaspoon ground cinnamon
- ¼ teaspoon vanilla extract

1. Insert the crisper plate into the basket and the basket into the unit. Preheat the unit by selecting BAKE, setting the temperature to 120ºC, and setting the time to 3 minutes. Select START/STOP to begin. 2. In a medium bowl, stir together the oats, maple syrup, sugar, oil, salt, cinnamon, and vanilla until thoroughly combined. Transfer the muesli to a 6-by-2-inch round baking pan. 3. Once the unit is preheated, place the pan into the basket. 4. Select BAKE, set the temperature to 120ºC and set the time to 40 minutes. Select START/STOP to begin. 5. After 10 minutes, stir the muesli well. Resume cooking, stirring the muesli every 10 minutes, for a total of 40 minutes, or until the muesli is lightly browned and mostly dry. 6. When the cooking is complete, place the muesli on a plate to cool. It will become crisp as it cools. Store the completely cooled muesli in an airtight container in a cool, dry place for 1 to 2 weeks.

Turkey Banger Breakfast Pizza

Prep time: 15 minutes | Cook time: 24 minutes | Serves 2

- 4 large eggs, divided
- 1 tablespoon water
- ½ teaspoon garlic powder
- ½ teaspoon onion granules
- ½ teaspoon dried oregano
- 2 tablespoons coconut flour
- 3 tablespoons grated Parmesan cheese
- 120 g grated low-moisture Mozzarella or other melting cheese
- 1 link cooked turkey banger, chopped (about 60 g)
- 2 sun-dried tomatoes, finely chopped
- 2 sping onions, thinly sliced

1. Preheat the air fryer to 200ºC. Line a cake pan with parchment paper and lightly coat the paper with rapeseed oil. 2. In a large bowl, whisk 2 of the eggs with the water, garlic powder, onion granules, and dried oregano. Add the coconut flour, breaking up any lumps with your hands as you add it to the bowl. Stir the coconut flour into the egg mixture, mixing until smooth. Stir in the Parmesan cheese. Allow the mixture to rest for a few minutes until thick and dough-like. 3. Transfer the mixture to the prepared pan. Use a spatula to spread it evenly and slightly up the sides of the pan. Air fry until the crust is set but still light in color, about 10 minutes. Top with the cheeses, banger, and sun-dried tomatoes. 4. Break the remaining 2 eggs into a small bowl, then slide them onto the pizza. Return the pizza to the air fryer. Air fry 10 to 14 minutes until the egg whites are set and the yolks are the desired doneness. Top with the spring onions and allow to rest for 5 minutes before serving.

Homemade Cherry Breakfast Tarts

Prep time: 15 minutes | Cook time: 20 minutes | Serves 6

Tarts:
- 2 refrigerated piecrusts
- 80 g cherry preserves

Frosting:
- 120 ml vanilla yoghurt
- 30 g soft cheese
- 1 teaspoon cornflour
- Cooking oil
- 1 teaspoon stevia
- Rainbow sprinkles

Make the Tarts 1. Place the piecrusts on a flat surface. Using a knife or pizza cutter, cut each piecrust into 3 rectangles, for 6 total. (I discard the unused dough left from slicing the edges.) 2. In a small bowl, combine the preserves and cornflour. Mix well. 3. Scoop 1 tablespoon of the preserves mixture onto the top half of each piece of piecrust. 4. Fold the bottom of each piece up to close the tart. Using the back of a fork, press along the edges of each tart to seal. 5. Spray the breakfast tarts with cooking oil and place them in the air fryer. I do not recommend stacking the breakfast tarts. They will stick together if stacked. You may need to prepare them in two batches. Bake at 190ºC for 10 minutes. 6. Allow the breakfast tarts to cool fully before removing from the air fryer. 7. If necessary, repeat steps 5 and 6 for the remaining breakfast tarts. Make the Frosting 8. In a small bowl, combine the yoghurt, soft cheese, and stevia. Mix well. 9. Spread the breakfast tarts with frosting and top with sprinkles, and serve.

Breakfast Cobbler

Prep time: 20 minutes | Cook time: 30 minutes | Serves 4

Filling:
- 280 g banger meat, crumbled
- 60 g minced onions
- 2 cloves garlic, minced
- ½ teaspoon fine sea salt
- ½ teaspoon ground black pepper
- 1 (230 g) package soft cheese (or soft cheese style spread for dairy-free), softened
- 180 g beef or chicken stock

Biscuits:
- 3 large egg whites
- 90 g blanched almond flour
- 1 teaspoon baking powder
- ¼ teaspoon fine sea salt
- 2½ tablespoons very cold unsalted butter, cut into ¼-inch pieces
- Fresh thyme leaves, for garnish

1. Preheat the air fryer to 200ºC. 2. Place the banger, onions, and garlic in a pie dish. Using your hands, break up the banger into small pieces and spread it evenly throughout the pie dish. Season with the salt and pepper. Place the pan in the air fryer and bake for 5 minutes. 3. While the banger cooks, place the soft cheese and stock in a food processor or blender and purée until smooth. 4. Remove the pork from the air fryer and use a fork or metal spatula to crumble it more. Pour the soft cheese mixture into the banger and stir to combine. Set aside. 5. Make the biscuits: Place the egg whites in a medium-sized mixing bowl or the bowl of a stand mixer and whip with a hand mixer or stand mixer until stiff peaks form. 6. In a separate medium-sized bowl, whisk together the almond flour, baking powder, and salt, then cut in the butter. When you are done, the mixture should still have chunks of butter. Gently fold the flour mixture into the egg whites with a rubber spatula. 7. Use a large spoon or ice cream scoop to scoop the dough into 4 equal-sized biscuits, making sure the butter is evenly distributed. Place the biscuits on top of the banger and cook in the air fryer for 5 minutes, then turn the heat down to 160ºC and bake for another 17 to 20 minutes, until the biscuits are golden brown. Serve garnished with fresh thyme leaves. 8. Store leftovers in an airtight container in the refrigerator for up to 3 days. Reheat in a preheated 180ºC air fryer for 5 minutes, or until warmed through.

Lemon-Blueberry Muffins

Prep time: 5 minutes | Cook time: 20 to 25 minutes | Makes 6 muffins

- 150 g almond flour
- 3 tablespoons granulated sweetener
- 1 teaspoon baking powder
- 2 large eggs
- 3 tablespoons melted butter
- 1 tablespoon almond milk
- 1 tablespoon fresh lemon juice
- 120 g fresh blueberries

1. Preheat the air fryer to 180°C. Lightly coat 6 silicone muffin cups with vegetable oil. Set aside. 2. In a large mixing bowl, combine the almond flour, sweetener, and baking soda. Set aside. 3. In a separate small bowl, whisk together the eggs, butter, milk, and lemon juice. Add the egg mixture to the flour mixture and stir until just combined. Fold in the blueberries and let the batter sit for 5 minutes. 4. Spoon the muffin batter into the muffin cups, about two-thirds full. Air fry for 20 to 25 minutes, or until a toothpick inserted into the center of a muffin comes out clean. 5. Remove the basket from the air fryer and let the muffins cool for about 5 minutes before transferring them to a wire rack to cool completely.

Apple Cider Doughnut Holes

Prep time: 10 minutes | Cook time: 6 minutes | Makes 10 mini doughnuts

Doughnut Holes:
- 175 g plain flour
- 2 tablespoons granulated sugar
- 2 teaspoons baking powder
- 1 teaspoon baking soda
- ½ teaspoon coarse or flaky salt

Glaze:
- 96 g icing sugar
- 2 tablespoons unsweetened apple sauce

- Pinch of freshly grated nutmeg
- 60 ml plus 2 tablespoons buttermilk, chilled
- 2 tablespoons apple cider or apple juice, chilled
- 1 large egg, lightly beaten
- Vegetable oil, for brushing

- ¼ teaspoon vanilla extract
- Pinch of coarse or flaky salt

1. Make the doughnut holes: In a bowl, whisk together the flour, granulated sugar, baking powder, baking soda, salt, and nutmeg until smooth. Add the buttermilk, cider, and egg and stir with a small rubber spatula or spoon until the dough just comes together. 2. Using a 28 g ice cream scoop or 2 tablespoons, scoop and drop 10 balls of dough into the air fryer basket, spaced evenly apart, and brush the tops lightly with oil. Air fry at 180°C until the doughnut holes are golden brown and fluffy, about 6 minutes. Transfer the doughnut holes to a wire rack to cool completely. 3. Make the glaze: In a small bowl, stir together the icing sugar, apple sauce, vanilla, and salt until smooth. 4. Dip the tops of the doughnuts holes in the glaze, then let stand until the glaze sets before serving. If you're impatient and want warm doughnuts, have the glaze ready to go while the doughnuts cook, then use the glaze as a dipping sauce for the warm doughnuts, fresh out of the air fryer.

Chapter 2

Family Favorites

Chapter 2 Family Favorites

Veggie Tuna Melts

Prep time: 15 minutes | Cook time: 7 to 11 minutes | Serves 4

- 2 low-salt wholemeal English muffins, split
- 1 (170 g) tin chunk light low-salt tuna, drained
- 235 g shredded carrot
- 80 g chopped mushrooms
- 2 spring onions, white and green parts, sliced
- 80 ml fat-free Greek yoghurt
- 2 tablespoons low-salt wholegrain mustard
- 2 slices low-salt low-fat Swiss cheese, halved

1. Place the English muffin halves in the air fryer basket. 2. Air fry at 170ºC for 3 to 4 minutes, or until crisp. Remove from the basket and set aside. 3. In a medium bowl, thoroughly mix the tuna, carrot, mushrooms, spring onions, yoghurt, and mustard. 4. Top each half of the muffins with one-fourth of the tuna mixture and a half slice of Swiss cheese. 5. Air fry for 4 to 7 minutes, or until the tuna mixture is hot and the cheese melts and starts to brown. 6. Serve immediately.

Pecan Rolls

Prep time: 20 minutes | Cook time: 20 to 24 minutes | Makes 12 rolls

- 220 g plain flour, plus more for dusting
- 2 tablespoons caster sugar, plus 60 ml, divided
- 1 teaspoon salt
- 3 tablespoons butter, at room temperature
- 180 ml milk, whole or semi-skimmed
- 40 g packed light muscovado sugar
- 120g chopped pecans, toasted
- 1 to 2 tablespoons oil
- 35g icing sugar (optional)

1. In a large bowl, whisk the flour, 2 tablespoons caster sugar, and salt until blended. 2. Stir in the butter and milk briefly until a sticky dough form. In a small bowl, stir together the brown sugar and remaining 60 g caster sugar. 3. Place a piece of parchment paper on a work surface and dust it with flour. Roll the dough on the prepared surface to ¼ inch thickness. 4. Spread the sugar mixture over the dough. Sprinkle the pecans on top. Roll up the dough jam roll-style, pinching the ends to seal. 5. Cut the dough into 12 rolls. Preheat the air fryer to 160ºC. 6. Line the air fryer basket with parchment paper and spritz the parchment with oil. Place 6 rolls on the prepared parchment. Bake for 5 minutes. 7. Flip the rolls and bake for 5 to 7 minutes more until lightly browned. Repeat with the remaining rolls. 8. Sprinkle with icing sugar (if using).

Personal Cauliflower Pizzas

Prep time: 10 minutes | Cook time: 25 minutes | Serves 2

- 1 (340 g) bag frozen riced cauliflower
- 75 g shredded Mozzarella cheese
- 15 g almond flour
- 20 g Parmesan cheese
- 1 large egg
- ½ teaspoon salt
- 1 teaspoon garlic powder
- 1 teaspoon dried oregano
- 4 tablespoons no-sugar-added marinara sauce, divided
- 110 g fresh Mozzarella, chopped, divided
- 140 g cooked chicken breast, chopped, divided
- 100 g chopped cherry tomatoes, divided
- 5 g fresh baby rocket, divided

1. Preheat the air fryer to 200ºC. Cut 4 sheets of parchment paper to fit the basket of the air fryer. Brush with olive oil and set aside. 2. In a large glass bowl, microwave the cauliflower according to package directions. Place the cauliflower on a clean towel, draw up the sides, and squeeze tightly over a sink to remove the excess moisture. Return the cauliflower to the bowl and add the shredded Mozzarella along with the almond flour, Parmesan, egg, salt, garlic powder, and oregano. Stir until thoroughly combined. 3. Divide the dough into two equal portions. Place one piece of dough on the prepared parchment paper and pat gently into a thin, flat disk 7 to 8 inches in diameter. Air fry for 15 minutes until the crust begins to brown. Let cool for 5 minutes. 4. Transfer the parchment paper with the crust on top to a baking sheet. Place a second sheet of parchment paper over the crust. While holding the edges of both sheets together, carefully lift the crust off the baking sheet, flip it, and place it back in the air fryer basket. The new sheet of parchment paper is now on the bottom. Remove the top piece of paper and air fry the crust for another 15 minutes until the top begins to brown. Remove the basket from the air fryer. 5. Spread 2 tablespoons of the marinara sauce on top of the crust, followed by half the fresh Mozzarella, chicken, cherry tomatoes, and rocket. Air fry for 5 to 10 minutes longer, until the cheese is melted and beginning to brown. Remove the pizza from the oven and let it sit for 10 minutes before serving. Repeat with the remaining ingredients to make a second pizza.

Beef Jerky

Prep time: 30 minutes | Cook time: 2 hours | Serves 8

- Oil, for spraying
- 450 g silverside, cut into thin, short slices
- 60 ml soy sauce
- 3 tablespoons packed light muscovado sugar
- 1 tablespoon minced garlic
- 1 teaspoon ground ginger
- 1 tablespoon water

1. Line the air fryer basket with parchment and spray lightly with oil. 2. Place the steak, soy sauce, brown sugar, garlic, ginger, and water in a zip-top plastic bag, seal, and shake well until evenly coated. 3. Refrigerate for 30 minutes. Place the steak in the prepared basket in a single layer. 4. You may need to work in batches, depending on the size of your air fryer. 5. Air fry at 80°C for at least 2 hours. 6. Add more time if you like your jerky a bit tougher.

Avocado and Egg Burrito

Prep time: 10 minutes | Cook time: 3 to 5 minutes | Serves 4

- 2 hard-boiled egg whites, chopped
- 1 hard-boiled egg, chopped
- 1 avocado, peeled, pitted, and chopped
- 1 red pepper, chopped
- 3 tablespoons low-salt salsa, plus additional for serving (optional)
- 1 (34 g) slice low-salt, low-fat processed cheese, torn into pieces
- 4 low-salt wholemeal flour wraps

1. In a medium bowl, thoroughly mix the egg whites, egg, avocado, red pepper, salsa, and cheese. 2. Place the maize wraps on a work surface and evenly divide the filling among them. 3. Fold in the edges and roll up. Secure the burritos with toothpicks if necessary. 4. Put the burritos in the air fryer basket. 5. Air fry at 200°C for 3 to 5 minutes, or until the burritos are light golden brown and crisp. 6. Serve with more salsa (if using).

Fish and Vegetable Tacos

Prep time: 15 minutes | Cook time: 9 to 12 minutes | Serves 4

- 450 g white fish fillets, such as sole or cod
- 2 teaspoons olive oil
- 3 tablespoons freshly squeezed lemon juice, divided
- 350 g chopped red cabbage
- 1 large carrot, grated
- 120 ml low-salt salsa
- 80 ml low-fat Greek yoghurt
- 4 soft low-salt wholemeal maize wraps

1. Brush the fish with the olive oil and sprinkle with 1 tablespoon of lemon juice. 2. Air fry in the air fryer basket at 200°C for 9 to 12 minutes, or until the fish just flakes when tested with a fork. 3. Meanwhile, in a medium bowl, stir together the remaining 2 tablespoons of lemon juice, the red cabbage, carrot, salsa, and yoghurt. 4. When the fish is cooked, remove it from the air fryer basket and break it up into large pieces. 5. Offer the fish, maize wraps, and the cabbage mixture, and let each person assemble a taco.

Old Bay Tilapia

Prep time: 15 minutes | Cook time: 6 minutes | Serves 4

- Oil, for spraying
- 235 ml panko breadcrumbs
- 2 tablespoons Old Bay or all-purpose seasoning
- 2 teaspoons granulated garlic
- 1 teaspoon onion powder
- ½ teaspoon salt
- ¼ teaspoon freshly ground black pepper
- 1 large egg
- 4 tilapia fillets

1. Preheat the air fryer to 204°C. Line the air fryer basket with parchment and spray lightly with oil. 2. In a shallow bowl, mix together the breadcrumbs, seasoning, garlic, onion powder, salt, and black pepper. 3. In a small bowl, whisk the egg. Coat the tilapia in the egg, then dredge in the bread crumb mixture until completely coated. 4. Place the tilapia in the prepared basket. You may need to work in batches, depending on the size of your air fryer. 5. Spray lightly with oil. Cook for 4 to 6 minutes, depending on the thickness of the fillets, until the internal temperature reaches 64°C. 6. Serve immediately.

Steak Tips and Potatoes

Prep time: 10 minutes | Cook time: 20 minutes | Serves 4

- Oil, for spraying
- 227 g baby potatoes, cut in half
- ½ teaspoon salt
- 450 g steak, cut into ½-inch pieces
- 1 teaspoon Worcester sauce
- 1 teaspoon garlic powder
- ½ teaspoon salt
- ½ teaspoon ground black pepper

1. Line the air fryer basket with parchment and spray lightly with oil. 2. In a microwave-safe bowl, combine the potatoes and salt, then pour in about ½ inch of water. 3. Microwave for 7 minutes, or until the potatoes are nearly tender. Drain. 4. In a large bowl, gently mix together the steak, potatoes, Worcester sauce, garlic, salt, and black pepper. 5. Spread the mixture in an even layer in the prepared basket. Air fry at 200°C for 12 to 17 minutes, stirring after 5 to 6 minutes. 6. The cooking time will depend on the thickness of the meat and preferred doneness.

Chinese-Inspired Spareribs

Prep time: 30 minutes | Cook time: 8 minutes | Serves 4

- Oil, for spraying
- 340 g pork ribs, cut into 3-inch-long pieces
- 235 ml soy sauce
- 140 g sugar
- 120 g beef broth
- 60 ml honey
- 2 tablespoons minced garlic
- 1 teaspoon ground ginger
- 2 drops red food dye (optional)

1. Line the air fryer basket with parchment and spray lightly with oil. 2.Combine the ribs, soy sauce, sugar, beef broth, honey, garlic, ginger, and food colouring (if using) in a large zip-top plastic bag, seal, and shake well until completely coated. 3.Refrigerate for at least 30 minutes. 4.Place the ribs in the prepared basket. 5.Air fry at 190°C for 8 minutes, or until the internal temperature reaches 74°C.

Bacon-Wrapped Hot Dogs

Prep time: 5 minutes | Cook time: 10 minutes | Serves 4

- Oil, for spraying
- 4 bacon rashers
- 4 hot dog bangers
- 4 hot dog rolls
- Toppings of choice

1. Line the air fryer basket with parchment and spray lightly with oil. 2.Wrap a strip of bacon tightly around each hot dog, taking care to cover the tips so they don't get too crispy. 3.Secure with a toothpick at each end to keep the bacon from shrinking. 4.Place the hot dogs in the prepared basket. 5.Air fry at 190°C for 8 to 9 minutes, depending on how crispy you like the bacon. For extra-crispy, cook the hot dogs at 200°C for 6 to 8 minutes. 6.Place the hot dogs in the buns, return them to the air fryer, and cook for another 1 to 2 minutes, or until the buns are warm. 7.Add your desired toppings and serve.

Chapter 2 Family Favorites

Chapter 3

Fast and Easy Everyday Favourites

Chapter 3 Fast and Easy Everyday Favourites

Crunchy Fried Okra

Prep time: 5 minutes | Cook time: 8 to 10 minutes | Serves 4

- 120 g self-raising yellow cornmeal (alternatively add 1 tablespoon baking powder to cornmeal)
- 1 teaspoon Italian-style seasoning
- 1 teaspoon paprika
- 1 teaspoon salt
- ½ teaspoon freshly ground black pepper
- 2 large eggs, beaten
- 475 g okra slices
- Cooking spray

1. Preheat the air fryer to 200°C. 2. Line the air fryer basket with parchment paper. In a shallow bowl, whisk the cornmeal, Italian-style seasoning, paprika, salt, and pepper until blended. 3. Place the beaten eggs in a second shallow bowl. Add the okra to the beaten egg and stir to coat. 4. Add the egg and okra mixture to the cornmeal mixture and stir until coated. 5. Place the okra on the parchment and spritz it with oil. 6. Air fry for 4 minutes. Shake the basket, spritz the okra with oil, and air fry for 4 to 6 minutes more until lightly browned and crispy. 7. Serve immediately.

Purple Potato Chips with Rosemary

Prep time: 10 minutes | Cook time: 9 to 14 minutes | Serves 6

- 235 ml Greek yoghurt
- 2 chipotle chillies, minced
- 2 tablespoons adobo or chipotle sauce
- 1 teaspoon paprika
- 1 tablespoon lemon juice
- 10 purple fingerling or miniature potatoes
- 1 teaspoon olive oil
- 2 teaspoons minced fresh rosemary leaves
- ⅛ teaspoon cayenne pepper
- ¼ teaspoon coarse sea salt

1. Preheat the air fryer to 200°C. 2. In a medium bowl, combine the yoghurt, minced chillies, adobo sauce, paprika, and lemon juice. Mix well and refrigerate. 3. Wash the potatoes and dry them with paper towels. 4. Slice the potatoes lengthwise, as thinly as possible. You tin use a mandoline, a vegetable peeler, or a very sharp knife. 5. Combine the potato slices in a medium bowl and drizzle with the olive oil; toss to coat. 6. Air fry the chips, in batches, in the air fryer basket, for 9 to 14 minutes. 7. Use tongs to gently rearrange the chips halfway during cooking time. 8. Sprinkle the chips with the rosemary, cayenne pepper, and sea salt. 9. Serve with the chipotle sauce for dipping.

Baked Halloumi with Greek Salsa

Prep time: 15 minutes | Cook time: 6 minutes | Serves 4

Salsa:
- 1 small shallot, finely diced
- 3 garlic cloves, minced
- 2 tablespoons fresh lemon juice
- 2 tablespoons extra-virgin olive oil
- 1 teaspoon freshly cracked black pepper
- Pinch of rock salt
- 120 ml finely diced English cucumber
- 1 plum tomato, deseeded and finely diced
- 2 teaspoons chopped fresh parsley
- 1 teaspoon snipped fresh dill
- 1 teaspoon snipped fresh oregano

Cheese:
- 227 g Halloumi cheese, sliced into ½-inch-thick pieces
- 1 tablespoon extra-virgin olive oil

1. Preheat the air fryer to 192°C. 2. For the salsa: Combine the shallot, garlic, lemon juice, olive oil, pepper, and salt in a medium bowl. Add the cucumber, tomato, parsley, dill, and oregano. Toss gently to combine; set aside. 3. For the cheese: Place the cheese slices in a medium bowl. Drizzle with the olive oil. Toss gently to coat. 4. Arrange the cheese in a single layer in the air fryer basket. Bake for 6 minutes. 5. Divide the cheese among four serving plates. Top with the salsa and serve immediately.

Southwest Corn and Pepper Roast

Prep time: 10 minutes | Cook time: 10 minutes | Serves 4

For the Corn:
- 350 g thawed frozen corn kernels
- 235 g mixed diced peppers
- 1 jalapeño, diced
- 235 g diced brown onion
- ½ teaspoon ancho chilli powder

For Serving:
- 60 g feta cheese
- 60 g chopped fresh coriander
- 1 tablespoon fresh lemon juice
- 1 teaspoon ground cumin
- ½ teaspoon rock salt
- Cooking spray

- 1 tablespoon fresh lemon juice

1. Preheat the air fryer to 190°C 2.Spritz the air fryer with cooking spray 3.Combine the ingredients for the corn in a large bowl 4.Stir to mix well 5.Pour the mixture into the air fryer 6.Air fry for 10 minutes or until the corn and peppers are soft 7.Shake the basket halfway through the cooking time 8.Transfer them onto a large plate, then spread with feta cheese and coriander 9.Drizzle with lemon juice and serve.

Herb-Roasted Veggies

Prep time: 10 minutes | Cook time: 14 to 18 minutes | Serves 4

- 1 red pepper, sliced
- 1 (230 g) package sliced mushrooms
- 235 g runner beans, cut into 2-inch pieces
- 80 g diced red onion
- 3 garlic cloves, sliced
- 1 teaspoon olive oil
- ½ teaspoon dried basil
- ½ teaspoon dried tarragon

1. Preheat the air fryer to 180°C. 2.In a medium bowl, mix the red pepper, mushrooms, runner beans, red onion, and garlic. 3.Drizzle with the olive oil. Toss to coat. 4.Add the herbs and toss again. Place the vegetables in the air fryer basket. 5.Roast for 14 to 18 minutes, or until tender. 6.Serve immediately.

Air Fried Shishito Peppers

Prep time: 5 minutes | Cook time: 5 minutes | Serves 4

- 230 g shishito or Padron peppers (about 24)
- 1 tablespoon olive oil
- Coarse sea salt, to taste
- Lemon wedges, for serving
- Cooking spray

1. Preheat the air fryer to 200°C. 2.Spritz the air fryer basket with cooking spray. 3.Toss the peppers with olive oil in a large bowl to coat well. Arrange the peppers in the preheated air fryer. 4.Air fryer for 5 minutes or until blistered and lightly charred. Shake the basket and sprinkle the peppers with salt halfway through the cooking time. 5.Transfer the peppers onto a plate and squeeze the lemon wedges on top before serving.

Beef Bratwursts

Prep time: 5 minutes | Cook time: 15 minutes | Serves 4

- 4 (85 g) beef bratwursts

1. Preheat the air fryer to 190ºC. Place the beef bratwursts in the air fryer basket and air fry for 15 minutes, turning once halfway through. Serve hot.

Traditional Queso Fundido

Prep time: 10 minutes | Cook time: 25 minutes | Serves 4

- 110 g fresh Mexican (or Spanish if unavailable) chorizo, casings removed
- 1 medium onion, chopped
- 3 cloves garlic, minced
- 235 g chopped tomato
- 2 jalapeños, deseeded and diced
- 2 teaspoons ground cumin
- 475 g shredded Oaxaca or Mozzarella cheese
- 120 ml half-and-half (60 g whole milk and 60 ml cream combined)
- Celery sticks or tortilla chips, for serving

1. Preheat the air fryer to 200ºC. 2.In a baking tray, combine the chorizo, onion, garlic, tomato, jalapeños, and cumin. Stir to combine. 3.Place the pan in the air fryer basket. 4.Air fry for 15 minutes, or until the banger is cooked, stirring halfway through the cooking time to break up the banger. 5.Add the cheese and half-and-half; stir to combine. 6.Air fry for 10 minutes, or until the cheese has melted. 7.Serve with celery sticks or maize wrap chips.

Air Fried Broccoli

Prep time: 5 minutes | Cook time: 6 minutes | Serves 1

- 4 egg yolks
- 60 g melted butter
- 240 g coconut flour
- Salt and pepper, to taste
- 475 g broccoli florets

1. Preheat the air fryer to 200ºC. In a bowl, whisk the egg yolks and melted butter together. 2.Throw in the coconut flour, salt and pepper, then stir again to combine well. 3.Dip each broccoli floret into the mixture and place in the air fryer basket. 4.Air fry for 6 minutes in batches if necessary. Take care when removing them from the air fryer and serve immediately.

Buttery Sweet Potatoes

Prep time: 5 minutes | Cook time: 10 minutes | Serves 4

- 2 tablespoons melted butter
- 1 tablespoon light brown sugar
- 2 sweet potatoes, peeled and cut into ½-inch cubes
- Cooking spray

1. Preheat the air fryer to 200ºC. 2.Line the air fryer basket with parchment paper. In a medium bowl, stir together the melted butter and brown sugar until blended. 3.Toss the sweet potatoes in the butter mixture until coated. Place the sweet potatoes on the parchment and spritz with oil. 4.Air fry for 5 minutes. Shake the basket, spritz the sweet potatoes with oil, and air fry for 5 minutes more until they're soft enough to cut with a fork. 5.Serve immediately.

Chapter 4

Snacks and Starters

Chapter 4 Snacks and Starters

Golden Salmon and Carrot Croquettes

Prep time: 15 minutes | Cook time: 10 minutes | Serves 6

- 2 egg whites
- 120 g almond flour
- 120 g panko breadcrumbs
- 450 g chopped salmon fillet
- 160 g grated carrots
- 2 tablespoons minced garlic cloves
- 120 g chopped onion
- 2 tablespoons chopped chives
- Cooking spray

1. Preheat the air fryer to 180ºC 2. Spritz the air fryer basket with cooking spray 3. Whisk the egg whites in a bowl 4. Put the flour in a second bowl 5. Pour the breadcrumbs in a third bowl 6. Set aside 7. Combine the salmon, carrots, garlic, onion, and chives in a large bowl 8. Stir to mix well 9. Form the mixture into balls with your hands 10. Dredge the balls into the flour, then egg, and then breadcrumbs to coat well 11. Arrange the salmon balls in the preheated air fryer and spritz with cooking spray 12. Air fry for 10 minutes or until crispy and browned 13. Shake the basket halfway through 14. Serve immediately.

Rosemary-Garlic Shoestring Fries

Prep time: 5 minutes | Cook time: 18 minutes | Serves 2

- 1 large russet potatoes or Maris Piper potato (about 340 g), scrubbed clean, and julienned
- 1 tablespoon mixed vegetables oil
- Leaves from 1 sprig fresh rosemary
- Rock salt and freshly ground black pepper, to taste
- 1 garlic clove, thinly sliced
- Flaky sea salt, for serving

1. Preheat the air fryer to 200ºC. 2. Place the julienned potatoes in a large colander and rinse under cold running water until the water runs clear. Spread the potatoes out on a double layer of kitchen roll and pat dry. 3. In a large bowl, combine the potatoes, oil, and rosemary. Season with rock salt and pepper and toss to coat evenly. Place the potatoes in the air fryer and air fry for 18 minutes, shaking the basket every 5 minutes and adding the garlic in the last 5 minutes of cooking, or until the fries are golden and crisp. 4. Transfer the fries to a plate and sprinkle with flaky sea salt while they're hot. Serve immediately.

Prawns Egg Rolls

Prep time: 15 minutes | Cook time: 10 minutes per batch | Serves 4

- 1 tablespoon mixed vegetables oil
- ½ head green or savoy cabbage, finely shredded
- 90 g grated carrots
- 240 ml canned bean sprouts, drained
- 1 tablespoon soy sauce
- ½ teaspoon sugar
- 1 teaspoon sesame oil
- 60 ml hoisin sauce
- Freshly ground black pepper, to taste
- 454 g cooked prawns, diced
- 30 g spring onions
- 8 egg roll wrappers (or use spring roll pastry)
- mixed vegetables oil
- Duck sauce

1. Preheat a large sauté pan over medium-high heat. Add the oil and cook the cabbage, carrots and bean sprouts until they start to wilt, about 3 minutes. Add the soy sauce, sugar, sesame oil, hoisin sauce and black pepper. Sauté for a few more minutes. Stir in the prawns and spring onions and cook until the mixed vegetables are just tender. Transfer the mixture to a colander in a bowl to cool. Press or squeeze out any excess water from the filling so that you don't end up with soggy egg rolls. 2. Make the egg rolls: Place the egg roll wrappers on a flat surface with one of the points facing towards you so they look like diamonds. Dividing the filling evenly between the eight wrappers, spoon the mixture onto the centre of the egg roll wrappers. Spread the filling across the centre of the wrappers from the left corner to the right corner but leave 2 inches from each corner empty. Brush the empty sides of the wrapper with a little water. Fold the bottom corner of the wrapper tightly up over the filling, trying to avoid making any air pockets. Fold the left corner in toward the centre and then the right corner toward the centre. It should now look like an packet. Tightly roll the egg roll from the bottom to the top open corner. Press to seal the egg roll together, brushing with a little extra water if need be. Repeat this technique with all 8 egg rolls. 3. Preheat the air fryer to 190ºC. 4. Spray or brush all sides of the egg rolls with mixed vegetables oil. Air fry four egg rolls at a time for 10 minutes, turning them over halfway through the cooking time. 5. Serve hot with duck sauce or your favourite dipping sauce.

Chapter 4 Snacks and Appetizers

Italian Rice Balls

Prep time: 20 minutes | Cook time: 10 minutes | Makes 8 rice balls

- 355 g cooked sticky rice
- ½ teaspoon Italian seasoning blend
- ¾ teaspoon salt, divided
- 8 black olives, pitted
- 28 g mozzarella cheese cheese, cut into tiny pieces (small enough to stuff into olives)
- 2 eggs
- 35 g Italian breadcrumbs
- 55 g panko breadcrumbs
- Cooking spray

1. Preheat air fryer to 200ºC. 2. Stuff each black olive with a piece of mozzarella cheese cheese. Set aside. 3. In a bowl, combine the cooked sticky rice, Italian seasoning blend, and ½ teaspoon of salt and stir to mix well. Form the rice mixture into a log with your hands and divide it into 8 equal portions. Mould each portion around a black olive and roll into a ball. 4. Transfer to the freezer to chill for 10 to 15 minutes until firm. 5. In a shallow dish, place the Italian breadcrumbs. In a separate shallow dish, whisk the eggs. In a third shallow dish, combine the panko breadcrumbs and remaining salt. 6. One by one, roll the rice balls in the Italian breadcrumbs, then dip in the whisked eggs, finally coat them with the panko breadcrumbs. 7. Arrange the rice balls in the air fryer basket and spritz both sides with cooking spray. 8. Air fry for 10 minutes until the rice balls are golden. Flip the balls halfway through the cooking time. 9. Serve warm.

Mushroom Tarts

Prep time: 15 minutes | Cook time: 38 minutes | Makes 15 tarts

- 2 tablespoons extra-virgin olive oil, divided
- 1 small white onion, sliced
- 227 g shiitake mushrooms, sliced
- ¼ teaspoon sea salt
- ¼ teaspoon freshly ground black pepper
- 60 ml dry white wine
- 1 sheet frozen puff pastry, thawed
- 95 g shredded Gruyère cheese
- Cooking oil spray
- 1 tablespoon thinly sliced fresh chives

1. Insert the crisper plate into the basket and the basket into the unit. Preheat the unit by selecting BAKE, setting the temperature to 150ºC, and setting the time to 3 minutes. Select START/STOP to begin. 2. In a heatproof bowl that fits into the basket, stir together 1 tablespoon of olive oil, the onion, and the mushrooms. 3. Once the unit is preheated, place the bowl into the basket. 4. Select BAKE, set the temperature to 150ºC, and set the time to 7 minutes. Select START/STOP to begin. 5. After about 2½ minutes, stir the mixed vegetables. Resume cooking. After another 2½ minutes, the mixed vegetables should be browned and tender. Season with the salt and pepper and add the wine. Resume cooking until the liquid evaporates, about 2 minutes. 6. When the cooking is complete, place the bowl on a heatproof surface. 7. Increase the air fryer temperature to 200ºC and set the time to 3 minutes. Select START/STOP to begin. 8. Unfold the puff pastry and cut it into 15 (3-by-3-inch) squares. Using a fork, pierce the dough and brush both sides with the remaining 1 tablespoon of olive oil. 9. Evenly distribute half the cheese among the puff pastry squares, leaving a ½-inch border around the edges. Divide the mushroom-onion mixture among the pastry squares and top with the remaining cheese. 10. Once the unit is preheated, spray the crisper plate with cooking oil. Working in batches, place 5 tarts into the basket; do not stack or overlap. 11. Select BAKE, set the temperature to 200ºC, and set the time to 8 minutes. Select START/STOP to begin. 12. After 6 minutes, check the tarts; if not yet golden, resume cooking for about 2 minutes more. 13. When the cooking is complete, remove the tarts and transfer to a a wire rack to cool. Repeat steps 10, 11, and 12 with the remaining tarts. 14. Serve garnished with the chives.

Spiralized Potato Nest with Tomato Tomato Ketchup

Prep time: 10 minutes | Cook time: 15 minutes | Serves 2

- 1 large russet potatoes or Maris Piper potato (about 340 g)
- 2 tablespoons mixed vegetables oil
- 1 tablespoon hot smoked paprika
- ½ teaspoon garlic powder
- Rock salt and freshly ground black pepper, to taste
- 120 ml canned chopped tomatoes
- 2 tablespoons apple cider vinegar
- 1 tablespoon dark brown sugar
- 1 tablespoon Worcestershire sauce
- 1 teaspoon mild hot sauce

1. Using a spiralizer, spiralize the potato, then place in a large colander. (If you don't have a spiralizer, cut the potato into thin ⅛-inch-thick matchsticks.) Rinse the potatoes under cold running water until the water runs clear. Spread the potatoes out on a double layer of kitchen roll and pat completely dry. 2. In a large bowl, combine the potatoes, oil, paprika, and garlic powder. Season with salt and pepper and toss to combine. Transfer the potatoes to the air fryer and air fry at 200ºC until the potatoes are browned and crisp, 15 minutes, shaking the basket halfway through. 3. Meanwhile, in a small blender, purée the tomatoes, vinegar, brown sugar, Worcestershire sauce, and hot sauce until smooth. Pour into a small saucepan or frying pan and simmer medium heat until reduced by half, 3 to 5 minutes. Pour the homemade tomato ketchup into a bowl and let cool. 4. Remove the spiralized potato nest from the air fryer and serve hot with the tomato ketchup.

Chapter 4 Snacks and Appetizers

Baked Spanakopita Dip

Prep time: 10 minutes | Cook time: 15 minutes | Serves 2

- Olive oil cooking spray
- 3 tablespoons olive oil, divided
- 2 tablespoons minced white onion
- 2 garlic cloves, minced
- 100 g fresh spinach
- 113 g soft white cheese, softened
- 113 g feta cheese cheese, divided
- Zest of 1 lemon
- ¼ teaspoon ground nutmeg
- 1 teaspoon dried fresh dill
- ½ teaspoon salt
- Pitta chips, carrot sticks, or sliced bread for serving (optional)

1. Preheat the air fryer to 180°C. Coat the inside of a 6-inch ramekin or baking dish with olive oil cooking spray. 2. In a large frying pan over medium heat, heat 1 tablespoon of the olive oil. Add the onion, then cook for 1 minute. 3. Add in the garlic and cook, stirring for 1 minute more. 4. Reduce the heat to low and mix in the spinach and water. Let this cook for 2 to 3 minutes, or until the spinach has wilted. Remove the frying pan from the heat. 5. In a medium-sized bowl, combine the soft white cheese, 57 g of the feta cheese, and the remaining 2 tablespoons of olive oil, along with the lemon zest, nutmeg, fresh dill, and salt. Mix until just combined. 6. Add the mixed vegetables to the cheese base and stir until combined. 7. Pour the dip mixture into the prepared ramekin and top with the remaining 57 g of feta cheese cheese. 8. Place the dip into the air fryer basket and cook for 10 minutes, or until heated through and bubbling. 9. Serve with pitta chips, carrot sticks, or sliced bread.

Cheese-Stuffed Blooming Onion

Prep time: 10 minutes | Cook time: 15 minutes | Serves 2

- 1 large brown onion (397 g)
- 1 tablespoon olive oil
- Rock salt and freshly ground black pepper, to taste
- 18 g plus 2 tablespoons panko breadcrumbs
- 22 g grated Parmesan cheese
- 3 tablespoons mayonnaise
- 1 tablespoon fresh lemon juice
- 1 tablespoon chopped fresh flat-leaf parsley parsley
- 2 teaspoons wholemeal Dijon mustard
- 1 garlic clove, minced

1. Place the onion on a cutting board and trim the top off and peel off the outer skin. Turn the onion upside down and use a paring knife, cut vertical slits halfway through the onion at ½-inch intervals around the onion, keeping the root intact. When you turn the onion right side up, it should open up like the petals of a flower. Drizzle the cut sides of the onion with the olive oil and season with salt and pepper. Place petal-side up in the air fryer and air fry at 180°C for 10 minutes. 2. Meanwhile, in a bowl, stir together the panko, Parmesan, mayonnaise, lemon juice, parsley, mustard, and garlic until incorporated into a smooth paste. 3. Remove the onion from the fryer and stuff the paste all over and in between the onion "petals." Return the onion to the air fryer and air fry at 190°C until the onion is tender in the centre and the bread crumb mixture is golden, about 5 minutes. Remove the onion from the air fryer, transfer to a plate, and serve hot.

Carrot Chips

Prep time: 15 minutes | Cook time: 8 to 10 minutes | Serves 4

- 1 tablespoon olive oil, plus more for greasing the basket
- 4 to 5 medium carrots, trimmed and thinly sliced
- 1 teaspoon seasoned salt

1. Preheat the air fryer to 200°C. Grease the air fryer basket with the olive oil. 2. Toss the carrot slices with 1 tablespoon of olive oil and salt in a medium-sized bowl until thoroughly coated. 3. Arrange the carrot slices in the greased basket. You may need to work in batches to avoid overcrowding. 4. Air fry for 8 to 10 minutes until the carrot slices are crisp-tender. Shake the basket once during cooking. 5. Transfer the carrot slices to a bowl and repeat with the remaining carrots. 6. Allow to cool for 5 minutes and serve.

Bacon-Wrapped A Pickled Gherkin Spear

Prep time: 10 minutes | Cook time: 8 minutes | Serves 4

- 8 to 12 slices bacon
- 60 g soft white cheese
- 40 g shredded mozzarella cheese cheese
- 8 fresh dill a pickled gherkin spears
- 120 ml ranch dressing

1. Lay the bacon slices on a flat surface. In a medium-sized bowl, combine the soft white cheese and mozzarella cheese. stir until thoroughly combined. Spread the cheese mixture over the bacon slices. 2. Place a a pickled gherkin spear on a bacon slice and roll the bacon around the gherkin in a spiral, ensuring the gherkin is fully covered. (You may need to use more than one slice of bacon per gherkin to fully cover the spear.) Fold in the ends to ensure the bacon stays put. Repeat to wrap all the pickled cucumbers. 3. Place the wrapped pickled cucumbers in the air fryer basket in a single layer. Set the air fryer to 200°C for 8 minutes, or until the bacon is fully cooked and crisp on the edges. 4. Serve the a pickled gherkin spears with ranch dressing on the side.

Crispy Chilli Chickpeas

Prep time: 5 minutes | Cook time: 15 minutes | Serves 4

- 1 (425 g) tin cooked chickpeas, drained and rinsed
- 1 tablespoon olive oil
- ¼ teaspoon salt
- ⅛ teaspoon chilli powder
- ⅛ teaspoon garlic powder
- ⅛ teaspoon paprika

1. Preheat the air fryer to 190ºC. 2. In a medium-sized bowl, toss all of the ingredients together until the chickpeas are well coated. 3. Pour the chickpeas into the air fryer and spread them out in a single layer. 4. Roast for 15 minutes, stirring once halfway through the cook time.

Jalapeño Poppers

Prep time: 10 minutes | Cook time: 20 minutes | Serves 4

- Oil, for spraying
- 227 g soft white cheese
- 177 ml gluten-free breadcrumbs, divided
- 2 tablespoons chopped fresh parsley
- ½ teaspoon granulated garlic
- ½ teaspoon salt
- 10 red chillis, halved and seeded

1. Line the air fryer basket with parchment and spray lightly with oil. 2. In a medium bowl, mix together the soft white cheese, half of the breadcrumbs, the parsley, garlic, and salt. 3. Spoon the mixture into the jalapeño halves. Gently press the stuffed jalapeños in the remaining breadcrumbs. 4. Place the stuffed jalapeños in the prepared basket. 5. Air fry at 188ºC for 20 minutes, or until the cheese is melted and the breadcrumbs are crisp and golden brown.

Fried Artichoke Hearts

Prep time: 10 minutes | Cook time: 12 minutes | Serves 10

- Oil, for spraying
- 3 (397 g) tins quartered artichokes, drained and patted dry
- 120 ml mayonnaise
- 180 g panko breadcrumbs
- 50 g grated Parmesan cheese
- Salt and freshly ground black pepper, to taste

1. Line the air fryer basket with baking paper and spray lightly with oil. 2. Place the artichokes on a plate. Put the mayonnaise and breadcrumbs in separate bowls. 3. Working one at a time, dredge each artichoke heart in the mayonnaise, then in the breadcrumbs to cover. 4. Place the artichokes in the prepared basket. You may need to work in batches, depending on the size of your air fryer. 5. Air fry at 190ºC for 10 to 12 minutes, or until crispy and golden. 6. Sprinkle with the Parmesan cheese and season with salt and black pepper. Serve immediately.

Crispy Green Tomato Slices

Prep time: 10 minutes | Cook time: 8 minutes | Makes 12 slices

- 60 g plain flour
- 1 egg
- 120 ml buttermilk
- 120 g cornmeal
- 120 g panko breadcrumbs
- 2 green tomatoes, cut into ¼-inch-thick slices, patted dry
- ½ teaspoon salt
- ½ teaspoon ground black pepper
- Cooking spray

1. Preheat the air fryer to 200ºC 2.Line the air fryer basket with parchment paper 3.Pour the flour in a bowl 4.Whisk the egg and buttermilk in a second bowl 5.Combine the cornmeal and panko breadcrumbs in a third bowl 6.Dredge the tomato slices in the bowl of flour first, then into the egg mixture, and then dunk the slices into the cornmeal mixture 7.Shake the excess off 8.Transfer the well-coated tomato slices in the preheated air fryer and sprinkle with salt and ground black pepper 9.Spritz the tomato slices with cooking spray 10.Air fry for 8 minutes or until crispy and lightly browned 11.Flip the slices halfway through the cooking time 12.Serve immediately.

Pickle Chips

Prep time: 30 minutes | Cook time: 12 minutes | Serves 4

- Oil, for spraying
- 40 g sliced fresh dill or 240 g sweet gherkins, drained
- 240 ml buttermilk
- 245 g plain flour
- 2 large eggs, beaten
- 110 g panko breadcrumbs
- ¼ teaspoon salt

1. Line the air fryer basket with baking paper and spray lightly with oil. 2. In a shallow dish, combine the pickled cucumbers and buttermilk and let soak for at least 1 hour, then drain. 3. Place the flour, beaten eggs, and breadcrumbs in separate bowls. 4. Coat each gherkin chip lightly in the flour, dip in the eggs, and dredge in the breadcrumbs. Be sure each one is evenly coated. 5. Place the gherkin crisps in the prepared basket, sprinkle with the salt, and spray lightly with oil. You may need to work in batches, depending on the size of your air fryer. 6. Air fry at 200ºC for 5 minutes, flip, and cook for another 5 to 7 minutes, or until crispy. Serve hot.

Shishito Peppers with Herb Dressing

Prep time: 10 minutes | Cook time: 6 minutes | Serves 2 to 4

- 170 g shishito or Padron peppers
- 1 tablespoon mixed vegetables oil
- Rock salt and freshly ground black pepper, to taste
- 120 ml mayonnaise
- 2 tablespoons finely chopped fresh basil leaves
- 2 tablespoons finely chopped fresh flat-leaf parsley parsley
- 1 tablespoon finely chopped fresh tarragon
- 1 tablespoon finely finely chopped fresh chives
- Finely grated zest of ½ lemon
- 1 tablespoon fresh lemon juice
- Flaky sea salt, for serving

1. Preheat the air fryer to 200ºC. 2. In a bowl, toss together the shishitos and oil to evenly coat and season with rock salt and black pepper. Transfer to the air fryer and air fry for 6 minutes, shaking the basket halfway through, or until the shishitos are blistered and lightly charred. 3. Meanwhile, in a small bowl, whisk together the mayonnaise, basil, parsley, tarragon, chives, lemon zest, and lemon juice. 4. Pile the peppers on a plate, sprinkle with flaky sea salt, and serve hot with the dressing.

Fried Dill Pickles with Buttermilk Dressing

Prep time: 45 minutes | Cook time: 8 minutes | Serves 6 to 8

Buttermilk Dressing:
- 60 ml buttermilk
- 60 g chopped spring onions
- 180 ml mayonnaise
- 120 ml sour cream
- ½ teaspoon cayenne pepper
- ½ teaspoon onion powder
- ½ teaspoon garlic powder

Fried Dill Pickles:
- 90 g plain flour
- 1 (900 g) jar kosher dill pickles, cut into 4 spears, drained
- 300 g panko breadcrumbs
- 1 tablespoon chopped chives
- 2 tablespoons chopped fresh dill
- Rock salt and ground black pepper, to taste
- 2 eggs, beaten with 2 tablespoons water
- Rock salt and ground black pepper, to taste
- Cooking spray

1. Preheat the air fryer to 200ºC 2.Combine the ingredients for the dressing in a bowl 3.Stir to mix well 4.Wrap the bowl in plastic and refrigerate for 30 minutes or until ready to serve 5.Pour the flour in a bowl and sprinkle with salt and ground black pepper 6.Stir to mix well 7.Put the breadcrumbs in a separate bowl 8.Pour the beaten eggs in a third bowl 9.Dredge the pickle spears in the flour, then into the eggs, and then into the panko to coat well 10.Shake the excess off 11.Arrange the pickle spears in a single layer in the preheated air fryer and spritz with cooking spray 12.Air fry for 8 minutes 13.Flip the pickle spears halfway through 14.Serve the pickle spears with buttermilk dressing.

Artichoke and Olive Pitta Flatbread

Prep time: 5 minutes | Cook time: 10 minutes | Serves 4

- 2 wholewheat pitta bread
- 2 tablespoons olive oil, divided
- 2 garlic cloves, minced
- ¼ teaspoon salt
- 120 g canned artichoke hearts, sliced
- 70 g Kalamata olives
- 30 g shredded Parmesan
- 55 g crumbled feta cheese
- Chopped fresh parsley, for garnish (optional)

1. Preheat the air fryer to 190ºC. 2. Brush each pitta with 1 tablespoon olive oil, then sprinkle the minced garlic and salt over the top. 3. Distribute the artichoke hearts, olives, and cheeses evenly between the two pitta bread, and place both into the air fryer to bake for 10 minutes. 4. Remove the pitta bread and cut them into 4 pieces each before serving. Sprinkle parsley over the top, if desired.

Crispy Breaded Beef Cubes

Prep time: 10 minutes | Cook time: 12 to 16 minutes | Serves 4

- 450 g sirloin tip, cut into 1-inch cubes
- 240 ml cheese pasta sauce
- 355 g soft breadcrumbs
- 2 tablespoons olive oil
- ½ teaspoon dried marjoram

1. Preheat the air fryer to 180ºC. 2. In a medium-sized bowl, toss the beef with the pasta sauce to coat. 3. In a shallow dish, combine the breadcrumbs, oil, and marjoram, and mix well. Drop the beef cubes, one at a time, into the bread crumb mixture to coat thoroughly. 4. Air fry the beef in two batches for 6 to 8 minutes, shaking the basket once during cooking time, until the beef is at least 63ºC and the outside is crisp and brown. 5. Serve hot.

Soft white cheese Stuffed Jalapeño Chillies Poppers

Prep time: 12 minutes | Cook time: 6 to 8 minutes | Serves 10

- 227 g soft white cheese, at room temperature
- 80 g panko breadcrumbs, divided
- 2 tablespoons fresh parsley, minced
- 1 teaspoon chilli powder
- 10 jalapeño chillies chillies, halved and seeded
- Cooking oil spray

1. In a small bowl, whisk the soft white cheese, 40 g of panko, the parsley, and chilli powder until combined. Stuff the cheese mixture into the jalapeño chillies halves. 2. Sprinkle the tops of the stuffed jalapeño chillies with the remaining 40 g of panko and press it lightly into the filling. 3. Insert the crisper plate into the basket and the basket into the unit. Preheat the unit by selecting AIR FRY, setting the temperature to 190ºC, and setting the time to 3 minutes. Select START/STOP to begin. 4. Once the unit is preheated, spray the crisper plate with cooking oil. Place the poppers into the basket. 5. Select AIR FRY, set the temperature to 190ºC, and set the time to 8 minutes. Select START/STOP to begin. 6. After 6 minutes, check the poppers. If they are softened and the cheese is melted, they are done. If not, resume cooking. 7. When the cooking is complete, serve warm.

Chapter 5

Poultry

Chapter 5 Poultry

Chicken and Gammon Meatballs with Dijon Sauce

Prep time: 10 minutes | Cook time: 15 minutes | Serves 4

Meatballs:
- 230 g gammon, diced
- 230 g chicken mince
- 110 g grated Swiss cheese
- 1 large egg, beaten
- 3 cloves garlic, minced
- 15 g chopped onions
- 1½ teaspoons sea salt
- 1 teaspoon ground black pepper
- Cooking spray

Dijon Sauce:
- 3 tablespoons Dijon mustard
- 2 tablespoons lemon juice
- 60 ml chicken broth, warmed
- ¾ teaspoon sea salt
- ¼ teaspoon ground black pepper
- Chopped fresh thyme leaves, for garnish

1. Preheat the air fryer to 200°C. Spritz the air fryer basket with cooking spray. 2. Combine the ingredients for the meatballs in a large bowl. Stir to mix well, then shape the mixture in twelve 1½-inch meatballs. 3. Arrange the meatballs in a single layer in the air fryer basket. Air fry for 15 minutes or until lightly browned. Flip the balls halfway through. You may need to work in batches to avoid overcrowding. 4. Meanwhile, combine the ingredients, except for the thyme leaves, for the sauce in a small bowl. Stir to mix well. 5. Transfer the cooked meatballs on a large plate, then baste the sauce over. Garnish with thyme leaves and serve.

Bacon-Wrapped Chicken Breasts Rolls

Prep time: 10 minutes | Cook time: 15 minutes | Serves 4

- 15 g chopped fresh chives
- 2 tablespoons lemon juice
- 1 teaspoon dried sage
- 1 teaspoon fresh rosemary leaves
- 15 g fresh parsley leaves
- 4 cloves garlic, peeled
- 1 teaspoon ground fennel
- 3 teaspoons sea salt
- ½ teaspoon red pepper flakes
- 4 (115 g) boneless, skinless chicken breasts, pounded to ¼ inch thick
- 8 slices bacon
- Sprigs of fresh rosemary, for garnish
- Cooking spray

1. Preheat the air fryer to 170°C. Spritz the air fryer basket with cooking spray. 2. Put the chives, lemon juice, sage, rosemary, parsley, garlic, fennel, salt, and red pepper flakes in a food processor, then pulse to purée until smooth. 3. Unfold the chicken breasts on a clean work surface, then brush the top side of the chicken breasts with the sauce. 4. Roll the chicken breasts up from the shorter side, then wrap each chicken rolls with 2 bacon slices to cover. Secure with toothpicks. 5. Arrange the rolls in the preheated air fryer, then cook for 10 minutes. Flip the rolls halfway through. 6. Increase the heat to 200°C and air fry for 5 more minutes or until the bacon is browned and crispy. 7. Transfer the rolls to a large plate. Discard the toothpicks and spread with rosemary sprigs before serving.

Greek Chicken Souvlaki

Prep time: 30 minutes | Cook time: 15 minutes | Serves 3 to 4

Chicken:
- Grated zest and juice of 1 lemon
- 2 tablespoons extra-virgin olive oil
- 1 tablespoon Greek souvlaki seasoning
- 450 g boneless, skinless chicken breast, cut into 2-inch chunks
- Vegetable oil spray

For Serving:
- Warm pita bread or hot cooked rice
- Sliced ripe tomatoes
- Sliced cucumbers
- Thinly sliced red onion
- Kalamata olives
- Tzatziki

1. For the chicken: In a small bowl, combine the lemon zest, lemon juice, olive oil, and souvlaki seasoning. Place the chicken in a gallon-size resealable plastic bag. Pour the marinade over chicken. Seal bag and massage to coat. Place the bag in a large bowl and marinate for 30 minutes, or cover and refrigerate up to 24 hours, turning the bag occasionally. 2. Place the chicken a single layer in the air fryer basket. Set the air fryer to 180°C for 10 minutes, turning the chicken and spraying with a little vegetable oil spray halfway through the cooking time. Increase the air fryer temperature to 200°C for 5 minutes to allow the chicken to crisp and brown a little. 3. Transfer the chicken to a serving platter and serve with pita bread or rice, tomatoes, cucumbers, onion, olives and tzatziki.

Indian Fennel Chicken

Prep time: 30 minutes | Cook time: 15 minutes | Serves 4

- 450 g boneless, skinless chicken thighs, cut crosswise into thirds
- 1 brown onion, cut into 1½-inch-thick slices
- 1 tablespoon coconut oil, melted
- 2 teaspoons minced fresh ginger
- 2 teaspoons minced garlic
- 1 teaspoon smoked paprika
- 1 teaspoon ground fennel
- 1 teaspoon garam masala
- 1 teaspoon ground turmeric
- 1 teaspoon kosher salt
- ½ to 1 teaspoon cayenne pepper
- Vegetable oil spray
- 2 teaspoons fresh lemon juice
- 5 g chopped fresh coriander or parsley

1. Use a fork to pierce the chicken all over to allow the marinade to penetrate better. 2. In a large bowl, combine the onion, coconut oil, ginger, garlic, paprika, fennel, garam masala, turmeric, salt, and cayenne. Add the chicken, toss to combine, and marinate at room temperature for 30 minutes, or cover and refrigerate for up to 24 hours. 3. Place the chicken and onion in the air fryer basket. (Discard remaining marinade.) Spray with some vegetable oil spray. Set the air fryer to 180°C for 15 minutes. Halfway through the cooking time, remove the basket, spray the chicken and onion with more vegetable oil spray, and toss gently to coat. At the end of the cooking time, use a meat thermometer to ensure the chicken has reached an internal temperature of 76°C. 4. Transfer the chicken and onion to a serving platter. Sprinkle with the lemon juice and coriander and serve.

Chicken Paillard

Prep time: 10 minutes | Cook time: 10 minutes | Serves 2

- 2 large eggs, room temperature
- 1 tablespoon water
- 20 g powdered Parmesan cheese or pork dust
- 2 teaspoons dried thyme leaves
- 1 teaspoon ground black pepper
- 2 (140 g) boneless, skinless chicken breasts, pounded to ½ inch thick
- Lemon Butter Sauce:
- 2 tablespoons unsalted butter, melted
- 2 teaspoons lemon juice
- ¼ teaspoon finely chopped fresh thyme leaves, plus more for garnish
- ⅛ teaspoon fine sea salt
- Lemon slices, for serving

1. Spray the air fryer basket with avocado oil. Preheat the air fryer to 200°C. 2. Beat the eggs in a shallow dish, then add the water and stir well. 3. In a separate shallow dish, mix together the Parmesan, thyme, and pepper until well combined. 4. One at a time, dip the chicken breasts in the eggs and let any excess drip off, then dredge both sides of the chicken in the Parmesan mixture. As you finish, set the coated chicken in the air fryer basket. 5. Roast the chicken in the air fryer for 5 minutes, then flip the chicken and cook for another 5 minutes, or until cooked through and the internal temperature reaches 76°C. 6. While the chicken cooks, make the lemon butter sauce: In a small bowl, mix together all the sauce ingredients until well combined. 7. Plate the chicken and pour the sauce over it. Garnish with chopped fresh thyme and serve with lemon slices. 8. Store leftovers in an airtight container in the refrigerator for up to 4 days. Reheat in a preheated 200°C air fryer for 5 minutes, or until heated through.

Golden Chicken Cutlets

Prep time: 15 minutes | Cook time: 15 minutes | Serves 4

- 2 tablespoons panko breadcrumbs
- 20 g grated Parmesan cheese
- ⅛ tablespoon paprika
- ½ tablespoon garlic powder
- 2 large eggs
- 4 chicken cutlets
- 1 tablespoon parsley
- Salt and ground black pepper, to taste
- Cooking spray

1. Preheat air fryer to 200°C. Spritz the air fryer basket with cooking spray. 2. Combine the breadcrumbs, Parmesan, paprika, garlic powder, salt, and ground black pepper in a large bowl. Stir to mix well. Beat the eggs in a separate bowl. 3. Dredge the chicken cutlets in the beaten eggs, then roll over the breadcrumbs mixture to coat well. Shake the excess off. 4. Transfer the chicken cutlets in the preheated air fryer and spritz with cooking spray. 5. Air fry for 15 minutes or until crispy and golden brown. Flip the cutlets halfway through. 6. Serve with parsley on top.

Chipotle Aioli Wings

Prep time: 5 minutes | Cook time: 25 minutes | Serves 6

- 900 g bone-in chicken wings
- ½ teaspoon salt
- ¼ teaspoon ground black pepper
- 2 tablespoons mayonnaise
- 2 teaspoons chipotle powder
- 2 tablespoons lemon juice

1. In a large bowl, toss wings in salt and pepper, then place into ungreased air fryer basket. Adjust the temperature to 200°C and air fry for 25 minutes, shaking the basket twice while cooking. Wings will be done when golden and have an internal temperature of at least 76°C. 2. In a small bowl, whisk together mayonnaise, chipotle powder, and lemon juice. Place cooked wings into a large serving bowl and drizzle with aioli. Toss to coat. Serve warm.

Chicken Pesto Parmigiana

Prep time: 10 minutes | Cook time: 23 minutes | Serves 4

- 2 large eggs
- 1 tablespoon water
- Fine sea salt and ground black pepper, to taste
- 45 g powdered Parmesan cheese
- 2 teaspoons Italian seasoning
- 4 (140 g) boneless, skinless chicken breasts or thighs, pounded to ¼ inch thick
- 65 g pesto
- 115 g shredded Mozzarella cheese
- Finely chopped fresh basil, for garnish (optional)
- Grape tomatoes, halved, for serving (optional)

1. Spray the air fryer basket with avocado oil. Preheat the air fryer to 200ºC. 2. Crack the eggs into a shallow baking dish, add the water and a pinch each of salt and pepper, and whisk to combine. In another shallow baking dish, stir together the Parmesan and Italian seasoning until well combined. 3. Season the chicken breasts well on both sides with salt and pepper. Dip one chicken breast in the eggs and let any excess drip off, then dredge both sides of the breast in the Parmesan mixture. Spray the breast with avocado oil and place it in the air fryer basket. Repeat with the remaining 3 chicken breasts. 4. Air fry the chicken in the air fryer for 20 minutes, or until the internal temperature reaches 76ºC and the breading is golden brown, flipping halfway through. 5. Dollop each chicken breast with ¼ of the pesto and top with the Mozzarella. Return the breasts to the air fryer and cook for 3 minutes, or until the cheese is melted. Garnish with basil and serve with halved grape tomatoes on the side, if desired. 6. Store leftovers in an airtight container in the refrigerator for up to 4 days. Reheat in a preheated 200ºC air fryer for 5 minutes, or until warmed through.

Chipotle Drumsticks

Prep time: 15 minutes | Cook time: 20 minutes | Serves 4

- 1 tablespoon tomato paste
- ½ teaspoon chipotle powder
- ¼ teaspoon apple cider vinegar
- ¼ teaspoon garlic powder
- 8 chicken drumsticks
- ½ teaspoon salt
- ⅛ teaspoon ground black pepper

1. In a small bowl, combine tomato paste, chipotle powder, vinegar, and garlic powder. 2. Sprinkle drumsticks with salt and pepper, then place into a large bowl and pour in tomato paste mixture. Toss or stir to evenly coat all drumsticks in mixture. 3. Place drumsticks into ungreased air fryer basket. Adjust the temperature to 200ºC and air fry for 25 minutes, turning drumsticks halfway through cooking. Drumsticks will be dark red with an internal temperature of at least 76ºC when done. Serve warm.

Buttermilk Breaded Chicken

Prep time: 7 minutes | Cook time: 20 to 25 minutes | Serves 4

- 125 g plain flour
- 2 teaspoons paprika
- Pinch salt
- Freshly ground black pepper, to taste
- 80 ml buttermilk
- 2 eggs
- 2 tablespoons extra-virgin olive oil
- 185 g bread crumbs
- 6 chicken pieces, drumsticks, breasts, and thighs, patted dry
- Cooking oil spray

1. In a shallow bowl, stir together the flour, paprika, salt, and pepper. 2. In another bowl, beat the buttermilk and eggs until smooth. 3. In a third bowl, stir together the olive oil and bread crumbs until mixed. 4. Dredge the chicken in the flour, dip in the eggs to coat, and finally press into the bread crumbs, patting the crumbs firmly onto the chicken skin. 5. Insert the crisper plate into the basket and the basket into the unit. Preheat the unit by selecting AIR FRY, setting the temperature to 190ºC, and setting the time to 3 minutes. Select START/STOP to begin. 6. Once the unit is preheated, spray the crisper plate with cooking oil. Place the chicken into the basket. 7. Select AIR FRY, set the temperature to 190ºC, and set the time to 25 minutes. Select START/STOP to begin. 8. After 10 minutes, flip the chicken. Resume cooking. After 10 minutes more, check the chicken. If a food thermometer inserted into the chicken registers 76ºC and the chicken is brown and crisp, it is done. Otherwise, resume cooking for up to 5 minutes longer. 9. When the cooking is complete, let cool for 5 minutes, then serve.

Breaded Turkey Cutlets

Prep time: 5 minutes | Cook time: 8 minutes | Serves 4

- 30 g whole wheat bread crumbs
- ¼ teaspoon paprika
- ¼ teaspoon salt
- ¼ teaspoon black pepper
- ⅛ teaspoon dried sage
- ⅛ teaspoon garlic powder
- 1 egg
- 4 turkey breast cutlets
- Chopped fresh parsley, for serving

1. Preheat the air fryer to 192ºC. 2. In a medium shallow bowl, whisk together the bread crumbs, paprika, salt, black pepper, sage, and garlic powder. 3. In a separate medium shallow bowl, whisk the egg until frothy. 4. Dip each turkey cutlet into the egg mixture, then into the bread crumb mixture, coating the outside with the crumbs. Place the breaded turkey cutlets in a single layer in the bottom of the air fryer basket, making sure that they don't touch each other. 5. Bake for 4 minutes. Turn the cutlets over, then bake for 4 minutes more, or until the internal temperature reaches 76ºC. Sprinkle on the parsley and serve.

Smoky Chicken Leg Quarters

Prep time: 30 minutes | Cook time: 23 to 27 minutes | Serves 6

- 120 ml avocado oil
- 2 teaspoons smoked paprika
- 1 teaspoon sea salt
- 1 teaspoon garlic powder
- ½ teaspoon dried rosemary
- ½ teaspoon dried thyme
- ½ teaspoon freshly ground black pepper
- 900 g bone-in, skin-on chicken leg quarters

1. In a blender or small bowl, combine the avocado oil, smoked paprika, salt, garlic powder, rosemary, thyme, and black pepper. 2. Place the chicken in a shallow dish or large zip-top bag. Pour the marinade over the chicken, making sure all the legs are coated. Cover and marinate for at least 2 hours or overnight. 3. Place the chicken in a single layer in the air fryer basket, working in batches if necessary. Set the air fryer to 200°C and air fry for 15 minutes. Flip the chicken legs, then reduce the temperature to 180°C. Cook for 8 to 12 minutes more, until an instant-read thermometer reads 70°C when inserted into the thickest piece of chicken. 4. Allow to rest for 5 to 10 minutes before serving.

Coconut Chicken Wings with Mango Sauce

Prep time: 15 minutes | Cook time: 20 minutes | Serves 4

- 16 chicken drumettes (party wings)
- 60 ml full-fat coconut milk
- 1 tablespoon sriracha
- 1 teaspoon onion powder
- 1 teaspoon garlic powder
- Salt and freshly ground black pepper, to taste
- 25 g shredded unsweetened coconut
- 30 g plain flour
- Cooking oil spray
- 165 g mango, cut into ½-inch chunks
- 15 g fresh coriander, chopped
- 25 g red onion, chopped
- 2 garlic cloves, minced
- Juice of ½ lime

1. Place the drumettes in a resealable plastic bag. 2. In a small bowl, whisk the coconut milk and sriracha. 3. Drizzle the drumettes with the sriracha–coconut milk mixture. Season the drumettes with the onion powder, garlic powder, salt, and pepper. Seal the bag. Shake it thoroughly to combine the seasonings and coat the chicken. Marinate for at least 30 minutes, preferably overnight, in the refrigerator. 4. When the drumettes are almost done marinating, in a large bowl, stir together the desiccated coconut and flour. 5. Dip the drumettes into the coconut-flour mixture. Press the flour mixture onto the chicken with your hands. 6. Insert the crisper plate into the basket and the basket into the unit. Preheat the unit by selecting AIR FRY, setting the temperature to 200°C, and setting the time to 3 minutes. Select START/STOP to begin. 7. Once the unit is preheated, spray the crisper plate and the basket with cooking oil. Place the drumettes in the air fryer. It is okay to stack them. Spray the drumettes with cooking oil, being sure to cover the bottom layer. 8. Select AIR FRY, set the temperature to 200°C, and set the time to 20 minutes. Select START/STOP to begin. 9. After 5 minutes, remove the basket and shake it to ensure all pieces cook through. Reinsert the basket to resume cooking. Remove and shake the basket every 5 minutes, twice more, until a food thermometer inserted into the drumettes registers 76°C. 10. When the cooking is complete, let the chicken cool for 5 minutes. 11. While the chicken cooks and cools, make the salsa. In a small bowl, combine the mango, coriander, red onion, garlic, and lime juice. Mix well until fully combined. Serve with the wings.

Buffalo Chicken Cheese Sticks

Prep time: 5 minutes | Cook time: 8 minutes | Serves 2

- 140 g shredded cooked chicken
- 60 ml buffalo sauce
- 220 g shredded Mozzarella cheese
- 1 large egg
- 55 g crumbled feta

1. In a large bowl, mix all ingredients except the feta. Cut a piece of parchment to fit your air fryer basket and press the mixture into a ½-inch-thick circle. 2. Sprinkle the mixture with feta and place into the air fryer basket. 3. Adjust the temperature to 200°C and air fry for 8 minutes. 4. After 5 minutes, flip over the cheese mixture. 5. Allow to cool 5 minutes before cutting into sticks. Serve warm.

Lemon Chicken with Garlic

Prep time: 5 minutes | Cook time: 20 to 25 minutes | Serves 4

- 8 bone-in chicken thighs, skin on
- 1 tablespoon olive oil
- 1½ teaspoons lemon-pepper seasoning
- ½ teaspoon paprika
- ½ teaspoon garlic powder
- ¼ teaspoon freshly ground black pepper
- Juice of ½ lemon

1. Preheat the air fryer to 180°C. 2. Place the chicken in a large bowl and drizzle with the olive oil. Top with the lemon-pepper seasoning, paprika, garlic powder, and freshly ground black pepper. Toss until thoroughly coated. 3. Working in batches if necessary, arrange the chicken in a single layer in the basket of the air fryer. Pausing halfway through the cooking time to turn the chicken, air fry for 20 to 25 minutes, until a thermometer inserted into the thickest piece registers 76°C. 4. Transfer the chicken to a serving platter and squeeze the lemon juice over the top.

Chicken Manchurian

Prep time: 10 minutes | Cook time: 20 minutes | Serves 2

- 450 g boneless, skinless chicken breasts, cut into 1-inch pieces
- 60 g ketchup
- 1 tablespoon tomato-based chilli sauce, such as Heinz
- 1 tablespoon soy sauce
- 1 tablespoon rice vinegar
- 2 teaspoons vegetable oil
- 1 teaspoon hot sauce, such as Tabasco
- ½ teaspoon garlic powder
- ¼ teaspoon cayenne pepper
- 2 spring onions, thinly sliced
- Cooked white rice, for serving

1. Preheat the air fryer to 180°C. 2. In a bowl, combine the chicken, ketchup, chilli sauce, soy sauce, vinegar, oil, hot sauce, garlic powder, cayenne, and three-quarters of the spring onions and toss until evenly coated. 3. Scrape the chicken and sauce into a metal cake pan and place the pan in the air fryer. Bake until the chicken is cooked through and the sauce is reduced to a thick glaze, about 20 minutes, flipping the chicken pieces halfway through. 4. Remove the pan from the air fryer. Spoon the chicken and sauce over rice and top with the remaining spring onions. Serve immediately.

Harissa-Rubbed Chicken

Prep time: 30 minutes | Cook time: 21 minutes | Serves 4

Harissa:
- 120 ml olive oil
- 6 cloves garlic, minced
- 2 tablespoons smoked paprika
- 1 tablespoon ground coriander
- 1 tablespoon ground cumin
- 1 teaspoon ground caraway
- 1 teaspoon kosher salt
- ½ to 1 teaspoon cayenne pepper

Chickens:
- 120 g yoghurt
- 2 small chickens, any giblets removed, split in half lengthwise

1. For the harissa: In a medium microwave-safe bowl, combine the oil, garlic, paprika, coriander, cumin, caraway, salt, and cayenne. Microwave on high for 1 minute, stirring halfway through the cooking time. (You tin also heat this on the stovetop until the oil is hot and bubbling. Or, if you must use your air fryer for everything, cook it in the air fryer at 180°C for 5 to 6 minutes, or until the paste is heated through.) 2. For the chicken: In a small bowl, combine 1 to 2 tablespoons harissa and the yoghurt. Whisk until well combined. Place the chicken halves in a resealable plastic bag and pour the marinade over. Seal the bag and massage until all of the pieces are thoroughly coated. Marinate at room temperature for 30 minutes or in the refrigerator for up to 24 hours. 3. Arrange the hen halves in a single layer in the air fryer basket. (If you have a smaller air fryer, you may have to cook this in two batches.) Set the air fryer to 200°C for 20 minutes. Use a meat thermometer to ensure the chickens have reached an internal temperature of 76°C.

Thai-Style Cornish Game Hens

Prep time: 30 minutes | Cook time: 20 minutes | Serves 4

- 20 g chopped fresh coriander leaves and stems
- 60 ml fish sauce
- 1 tablespoon soy sauce
- 1 serrano chilli, seeded and chopped
- 8 garlic cloves, smashed
- 2 tablespoons sugar
- 2 tablespoons lemongrass paste
- 2 teaspoons black pepper
- 2 teaspoons ground coriander
- 1 teaspoon kosher salt
- 1 teaspoon ground turmeric
- 2 Cornish game hens, giblets removed, split in half lengthwise

1. In a blender, combine the coriander, fish sauce, soy sauce, serrano, garlic, sugar, lemongrass, black pepper, coriander, salt, and turmeric. Blend until smooth. 2. Place the game hen halves in a large bowl. Pour the coriander mixture over the hen halves and toss to coat. Marinate at room temperature for 30 minutes, or cover and refrigerate for up to 24 hours. 3. Arrange the hen halves in a single layer in the air fryer basket. Set the air fryer to 200°C for 20 minutes. Use a meat thermometer to ensure the game hens have reached an internal temperature of 76°C.

Cornish Hens with Honey-Lime Glaze

Prep time: 15 minutes | Cook time: 25 to 30 minutes | Serves 2 to 3

- 1 small chicken (680 to 900 g)
- 1 tablespoon honey
- 1 tablespoon lime juice
- 1 teaspoon poultry seasoning
- Salt and pepper, to taste
- Cooking spray

1. To split the chicken into halves, cut through breast bone and down one side of the backbone. 2. Mix the honey, lime juice, and poultry seasoning together and brush or rub onto all sides of the chicken. Season to taste with salt and pepper. 3. Spray the air fryer basket with cooking spray and place hen halves in the basket, skin-side down. 4. Air fry at 170°C for 25 to 30 minutes. Chicken will be done when juices run clear when pierced at leg joint with a fork. Let chicken rest for 5 to 10 minutes before cutting.

Chicken Legs with Leeks

Prep time: 30 minutes | Cook time: 18 minutes | Serves 6

- 2 leeks, sliced
- 2 large-sized tomatoes, chopped
- 3 cloves garlic, minced
- ½ teaspoon dried oregano
- 6 chicken legs, boneless and skinless
- ½ teaspoon smoked cayenne pepper
- 2 tablespoons olive oil
- A freshly ground nutmeg

1. In a mixing dish, thoroughly combine all ingredients, minus the leeks. Place in the refrigerator and let it marinate overnight. 2. Lay the leeks onto the bottom of the air fryer basket. Top with the chicken legs. 3. Roast chicken legs at (190°C for 18 minutes, turning halfway through. Serve with hoisin sauce.

Lettuce-Wrapped Turkey and Mushroom Meatballs

Prep time: 10 minutes | Cook time: 15 minutes | Serves 6

Sauce:
- 2 tablespoons tamari
- 2 tablespoons tomato sauce
- 1 tablespoon lime juice
- ¼ teaspoon peeled and grated fresh ginger
- 1 clove garlic, smashed to a paste
- 120 ml chicken broth
- 55 g sugar
- 2 tablespoons toasted sesame oil
- Cooking spray

Meatballs:
- 900 g turkey mince
- 75 g finely chopped button mushrooms
- 2 large eggs, beaten
- 1½ teaspoons tamari
- 15 g finely chopped spring onions, plus more for garnish
- 2 teaspoons peeled and grated fresh ginger
- 1 clove garlic, smashed
- 2 teaspoons toasted sesame oil
- 2 tablespoons sugar

For Serving:
- Lettuce leaves, for serving
- Sliced red chilies, for garnish (optional)
- Toasted sesame seeds, for garnish (optional)

1. Preheat the air fryer to 180°C. Spritz a baking pan with cooking spray. 2. Combine the ingredients for the sauce in a small bowl. Stir to mix well. Set aside. 3. Combine the ingredients for the meatballs in a large bowl. Stir to mix well, then shape the mixture in twelve 1½-inch meatballs. 4. Arrange the meatballs in a single layer on the baking pan, then baste with the sauce. You may need to work in batches to avoid overcrowding. 5. Arrange the pan in the air fryer. Air fry for 15 minutes or until the meatballs are golden brown. Flip the balls halfway through the cooking time. 6. Unfold the lettuce leaves on a large serving plate, then transfer the cooked meatballs on the leaves. Spread the red chilies and sesame seeds over the balls, then serve.

Chicken Patties

Prep time: 15 minutes | Cook time: 12 minutes | Serves 4

- 450 g chicken thigh mince
- 110 g shredded Mozzarella cheese
- 1 teaspoon dried parsley
- ½ teaspoon garlic powder
- ¼ teaspoon onion powder
- 1 large egg
- 60 g pork rinds, finely ground

1. In a large bowl, mix chicken mince, Mozzarella, parsley, garlic powder, and onion powder. Form into four patties. 2. Place patties in the freezer for 15 to 20 minutes until they begin to firm up. 3. Whisk egg in a medium bowl. Place the ground pork rinds into a large bowl. 4. Dip each chicken patty into the egg and then press into pork rinds to fully coat. Place patties into the air fryer basket. 5. Adjust the temperature to 180°C and air fry for 12 minutes. 6. Patties will be firm and cooked to an internal temperature of 76°C when done. Serve immediately.

Nacho Chicken Fries

Prep time: 20 minutes | Cook time: 6 to 7 minutes per batch | Serves 4 to 6

- 450 g chicken tenders
- Salt, to taste
- 15 g flour
- 2 eggs
- 45 g panko bread crumbs

Seasoning Mix:
- 1 tablespoon chilli powder
- 1 teaspoon ground cumin
- 20 g crushed organic nacho cheese maize wrap chips
- Oil for misting or cooking spray
- ½ teaspoon garlic powder
- ½ teaspoon onion powder

1. Stir together all seasonings in a small cup and set aside. 2. Cut chicken tenders in half crosswise, then cut into strips no wider than about ½ inch. 3. Preheat the air fryer to 200°C. 4. Salt chicken to taste. Place strips in large bowl and sprinkle with 1 tablespoon of the seasoning mix. Stir well to distribute seasonings. 5. Add flour to chicken and stir well to coat all sides. 6. Beat eggs together in a shallow dish. 7. In a second shallow dish, combine the panko, crushed chips, and the remaining 2 teaspoons of seasoning mix. 8. Dip chicken strips in eggs, then roll in crumbs. Mist with oil or cooking spray. 9. Chicken strips will cook best if done in two batches. They tin be crowded and overlapping a little but not stacked in double or triple layers. 10. Cook for 4 minutes. Shake basket, mist with oil, and cook 2 to 3 more minutes, until chicken juices run clear and outside is crispy. 11. Repeat step 10 to cook remaining chicken fries.

Chapter 5 Poultry

Buttermilk-Fried Drumsticks

Prep time: 10 minutes | Cook time: 25 minutes | Serves 2

- 1 egg
- 120 g buttermilk
- 45 g self-rising flour
- 45 g seasoned panko bread crumbs
- 1 teaspoon salt
- ¼ teaspoon ground black pepper (to mix into coating)
- 4 chicken drumsticks, skin on
- Oil for misting or cooking spray

1. Beat together egg and buttermilk in shallow dish. 2. In a second shallow dish, combine the flour, panko crumbs, salt, and pepper. 3. Sprinkle chicken legs with additional salt and pepper to taste. 4. Dip legs in buttermilk mixture, then roll in panko mixture, pressing in crumbs to make coating stick. Mist with oil or cooking spray. 5. Spray the air fryer basket with cooking spray. 6. Cook drumsticks at 180°C for 10 minutes. Turn pieces over and cook an additional 10 minutes. 7. Turn pieces to check for browning. If you have any white spots that haven't begun to brown, spritz them with oil or cooking spray. Continue cooking for 5 more minutes or until crust is golden brown and juices run clear. Larger, meatier drumsticks will take longer to cook than small ones.

French Garlic Chicken

Prep time: 30 minutes | Cook time: 27 minutes | Serves 4

- 2 tablespoon extra-virgin olive oil
- 1 tablespoon Dijon mustard
- 1 tablespoon apple cider vinegar
- 3 cloves garlic, minced
- 2 teaspoons herbes de Provence
- ½ teaspoon kosher salt
- 1 teaspoon black pepper
- 450 g boneless, skinless chicken thighs, halved crosswise
- 2 tablespoons butter
- 8 cloves garlic, chopped
- 60 g heavy whipping cream

1. In a small bowl, combine the olive oil, mustard, vinegar, minced garlic, herbes de Provence, salt, and pepper. Use a wire whisk to emulsify the mixture. 2. Pierce the chicken all over with a fork to allow the marinade to penetrate better. Place the chicken in a resealable plastic bag, pour the marinade over, and seal. Massage until the chicken is well coated. Marinate at room temperature for 30 minutes or in the refrigerator for up to 24 hours. 3. When you are ready to cook, place the butter and chopped garlic in a baking pan and place it in the air fryer basket. Set the air fryer to 200°C for 5 minutes, or until the butter has melted and the garlic is sizzling. 4. Add the chicken and the marinade to the seasoned butter. Set the air fryer to 180°C for 15 minutes. Use a meat thermometer to ensure the chicken has reached an internal temperature of 76°C. Transfer the chicken to a plate and cover lightly with foil to keep warm. 5. Add the cream to the pan, stirring to combine with the garlic, butter, and cooking juices. Place the pan in the air fryer basket. Set the air fryer to 180°C for 7 minutes. 6. Pour the thickened sauce over the chicken and serve.

Pecan Turkey Cutlets

Prep time: 10 minutes | Cook time: 10 to 12 minutes per batch | Serves 4

- 45 g panko bread crumbs
- ¼ teaspoon salt
- ¼ teaspoon pepper
- ¼ teaspoon mustard powder
- ¼ teaspoon poultry seasoning
- 50 g pecans
- 15 g cornflour
- 1 egg, beaten
- 450 g turkey cutlets, ½-inch thick
- Salt and pepper, to taste
- Oil for misting or cooking spray

1. Place the panko crumbs, ¼ teaspoon salt, ¼ teaspoon pepper, mustard, and poultry seasoning in food processor. Process until crumbs are finely crushed. Add pecans and process in short pulses just until nuts are finely chopped. Go easy so you don't overdo it! 2. Preheat the air fryer to 180°C. 3. Place cornflour in one shallow dish and beaten egg in another. Transfer coating mixture from food processor into a third shallow dish. 4. Sprinkle turkey cutlets with salt and pepper to taste. 5. Dip cutlets in cornflour and shake off excess. Then dip in beaten egg and roll in crumbs, pressing to coat well. Spray both sides with oil or cooking spray. 6. Place 2 cutlets in air fryer basket in a single layer and cook for 10 to 12 minutes or until juices run clear. 7. Repeat step 6 to cook remaining cutlets.

Crunchy Chicken Tenders

Prep time: 5 minutes | Cook time: 12 minutes | Serves 4

- 1 egg
- 60 ml unsweetened almond milk
- 15 g whole wheat flour
- 15 g whole wheat bread crumbs
- ½ teaspoon salt
- ½ teaspoon black pepper
- ½ teaspoon dried thyme
- ½ teaspoon dried sage
- ½ teaspoon garlic powder
- 450 g chicken tenderloins
- 1 lemon, quartered

1. Preheat the air fryer to 184°C. 2. In a shallow bowl, beat together the egg and almond milk until frothy. 3. In a separate shallow bowl, whisk together the flour, bread crumbs, salt, pepper, thyme, sage, and garlic powder. 4. Dip each chicken tenderloin into the egg mixture, then into the bread crumb mixture, coating the outside with the crumbs. Place the breaded chicken tenderloins into the bottom of the air fryer basket in an even layer, making sure that they don't touch each other. 5. Cook for 6 minutes, then turn and cook for an additional 5 to 6 minutes. Serve with lemon slices.

Sweet and Spicy Turkey Meatballs

Prep time: 15 minutes | Cook time: 15 minutes | Serves 6

- Olive oil
- 450 g lean turkey mince
- 30 g whole-wheat panko bread crumbs
- 1 egg, beaten
- 1 tablespoon soy sauce
- 60 ml plus 1 tablespoon hoisin sauce, divided
- 2 teaspoons minced garlic
- ⅛ teaspoon salt
- ⅛ teaspoon freshly ground black pepper
- 1 teaspoon Sriracha

1. Spray the air fryer basket lightly with olive oil. 2. In a large bowl, mix together the turkey, panko bread crumbs, egg, soy sauce, 1 tablespoon of hoisin sauce, garlic, salt, and black pepper. 3. Using a tablespoon, form 24 meatballs. 4. In a small bowl, combine the remaining 60 ml of hoisin sauce and Sriracha to make a glaze and set aside. 5. Place the meatballs in the air fryer basket in a single layer. You may need to cook them in batches. 6. Air fry at 180°C for 8 minutes. Brush the meatballs generously with the glaze and cook until cooked through, an additional 4 to 7 minutes.

Crispy Duck with Cherry Sauce

Prep time: 10 minutes | Cook time: 33 minutes | Serves 2 to 4

- 1 whole duck (2.3 kg), split in half, back and rib bones removed
- 1 teaspoon olive oil
- Salt and freshly ground black pepper, to taste

Cherry Sauce:
- 1 tablespoon butter
- 1 shallot, minced
- 120 ml sherry
- 240 g cherry preserves
- 240 ml chicken stock
- 1 teaspoon white wine vinegar
- 1 teaspoon fresh thyme leaves
- Salt and freshly ground black pepper, to taste

1. Preheat the air fryer to 200°C. 2. Trim some of the fat from the duck. Rub olive oil on the duck and season with salt and pepper. Place the duck halves in the air fryer basket, breast side up and facing the centre of the basket. 3. Air fry the duck for 20 minutes. Turn the duck over and air fry for another 6 minutes. 4. While duck is air frying, make the cherry sauce. Melt the butter in a large sauté pan. Add the shallot and sauté until it is just starting to brown, about 2 to 3 minutes. Add the sherry and deglaze the pan by scraping up any brown bits from the bottom of the pan. Simmer the liquid for a few minutes, until it has reduced by half. Add the cherry preserves, chicken stock and white wine vinegar. Whisk well to combine all the ingredients. Simmer the sauce until it thickens and coats the back of a spoon, about 5 to 7 minutes. Season with salt and pepper and stir in the fresh thyme leaves. 5. When the air fryer timer goes off, spoon some cherry sauce over the duck and continue to air fry at 200°C for 4 more minutes. Then, turn the duck halves back over so that the breast side is facing up. Spoon more cherry sauce over the top of the duck, covering the skin completely. Air fry for 3 more minutes and then remove the duck to a plate to rest for a few minutes. 6. Serve the duck in halves, or cut each piece in half again for a smaller serving. Spoon any additional sauce over the duck or serve it on the side.

Easy Cajun Chicken Drumsticks

Prep time: 5 minutes | Cook time: 40 minutes | Serves 5

- 1 tablespoon olive oil
- 10 chicken drumsticks
- 1½ tablespoons Cajun seasoning
- Salt and ground black pepper, to taste

1. Preheat the air fryer to 200°C. Grease the air fryer basket with olive oil. 2. On a clean work surface, rub the chicken drumsticks with Cajun seasoning, salt, and ground black pepper. 3. Arrange the seasoned chicken drumsticks in a single layer in the air fryer. You need to work in batches to avoid overcrowding. 4. Air fry for 18 minutes or until lightly browned. Flip the drumsticks halfway through. 5. Remove the chicken drumsticks from the air fryer. Serve immediately.

Chapter 6

Beef, Pork, and Lamb

Chapter 6 Beef, Pork, and Lamb

Teriyaki Rump Steak with Broccoli and Capsicum

Prep time: 5 minutes | Cook time: 13 minutes | Serves 4

- 230 g rump steak
- 80 ml teriyaki marinade
- 1½ teaspoons sesame oil
- ½ head broccoli, cut into florets
- 2 red peppers, sliced
- Fine sea salt and ground black pepper, to taste
- Cooking spray

1. Toss the rump steak in a large bowl with teriyaki marinade. Wrap the bowl in plastic and refrigerate to marinate for at least an hour. 2. Preheat the air fryer to 200ºC and spritz with cooking spray. 3. Discard the marinade and transfer the steak in the preheated air fryer. Spritz with cooking spray. 4. Air fry for 13 minutes or until well browned. Flip the steak halfway through. 5. Meanwhile, heat the sesame oil in a nonstick frying pan over medium heat. Add the broccoli and red pepper. Sprinkle with salt and ground black pepper. Sauté for 5 minutes or until the broccoli is tender. 6. Transfer the air fried rump steak on a plate and top with the sautéed broccoli and pepper. Serve hot.

Pork Chops with Caramelized Onions

Prep time: 20 minutes | Cook time: 23 to 34 minutes | Serves 4

- 4 bone-in pork chops (230 g each)
- 1 to 2 tablespoons oil
- 2 tablespoons Cajun seasoning, divided
- 1 brown onion, thinly sliced
- 1 green pepper, thinly sliced
- 2 tablespoons light brown sugar

1. Spritz the pork chops with oil. Sprinkle 1 tablespoon of Cajun seasoning on one side of the chops. 2. Preheat the air fryer to 200ºC. Line the air fryer basket with parchment paper and spritz the parchment with oil. 3. Place 2 pork chops, spice-side up, on the paper. 4. Cook for 4 minutes. Flip the chops, sprinkle with the remaining 1 tablespoon of Cajun seasoning, and cook for 4 to 8 minutes more until the internal temperature reaches 64ºC, depending on the chops' thickness. Remove and keep warm while you cook the remaining 2 chops. Set the chops aside. 5. In a baking tray, combine the onion, pepper, and brown sugar, stirring until the vegetables are coated. Place the pan in the air fryer basket and cook for 4 minutes. 6. Stir the vegetables. Cook for 3 to 6 minutes more to your desired doneness. Spoon the vegetable mixture over the chops to serve.

Spice-Coated Steaks with Cucumber and Snap Pea Salad

Prep time: 15 minutes | Cook time: 15 to 20 minutes | Serves 4

- 1 (680 g) boneless rump steak, trimmed and halved crosswise
- 1½ teaspoons chilli powder
- 1½ teaspoons ground cumin
- ¾ teaspoon ground coriander
- ⅛ teaspoon cayenne pepper
- ⅛ teaspoon ground cinnamon
- 1¼ teaspoons plus ⅛ teaspoon salt, divided
- ½ teaspoon plus ⅛ teaspoon ground black pepper, divided
- 1 teaspoon plus 1½ tablespoons extra-virgin olive oil, divided
- 3 tablespoons mayonnaise
- 1½ tablespoons white wine vinegar
- 1 tablespoon minced fresh dill
- 1 small garlic clove, minced
- 230 g sugar snap peas, strings removed and cut in half on bias
- ½ cucumber, halved lengthwise and sliced thin
- 2 radishes, trimmed, halved and sliced thin
- 475 g baby rocket

1. Preheat the air fryer to 200ºC. 2. In a bowl, mix chilli powder, cumin, coriander, cayenne pepper, cinnamon, 1¼ teaspoons salt and ½ teaspoon pepper until well combined. 3. Add the steaks to another bowl and pat dry with paper towels. Brush with 1 teaspoon oil and transfer to the bowl of spice mixture. Roll over to coat thoroughly. 4. Arrange the coated steaks in the air fryer basket, spaced evenly apart. Air fry for 15 to 20 minutes, or until an instant-read thermometer inserted in the thickest part of the meat registers at least 64ºC. Flip halfway through to ensure even cooking. 5. Transfer the steaks to a clean work surface and wrap with aluminium foil. Let stand while preparing salad. 6. Make the salad: In a large bowl, stir together 1½ tablespoons olive oil, mayonnaise, vinegar, dill, garlic, ⅛ teaspoon salt, and ⅛ teaspoon pepper. Add snap peas, cucumber, radishes and rocket. Toss to blend well. 7. Slice the steaks and serve with the salad.

Kheema Burgers

Prep time: 15 minutes | Cook time: 12 minutes | Serves 4

Burgers:
- 450 g 85% lean beef mince or lamb mince
- 2 large eggs, lightly beaten
- 1 medium brown onion, diced
- 60 g chopped fresh coriander
- 1 tablespoon minced fresh ginger
- 3 cloves garlic, minced
- 2 teaspoons garam masala
- 1 teaspoon ground turmeric
- ½ teaspoon ground cinnamon
- ⅛ teaspoon ground cardamom
- 1 teaspoon coarse or flaky salt
- 1 teaspoon cayenne pepper

Raita Sauce:
- 235 g grated cucumber
- 120 ml sour cream
- ¼ teaspoon coarse or flaky salt
- ¼ teaspoon black pepper

For Serving:
- 4 lettuce leaves, hamburger buns, or naan breads

1. For the burgers: In a large bowl, combine the beef mince, eggs, onion, coriander, ginger, garlic, garam masala, turmeric, cinnamon, cardamom, salt, and cayenne. Gently mix until ingredients are thoroughly combined. 2. Divide the meat into four portions and form into round patties. Make a slight depression in the middle of each patty with your thumb to prevent them from puffing up into a dome shape while cooking. 3. Place the patties in the air fryer basket. Set the air fryer to 180ºC for 12 minutes. Use a meat thermometer to ensure the burgers have reached an internal temperature of 72ºC (for medium). 4. Meanwhile, for the sauce: In a small bowl, combine the cucumber, sour cream, salt, and pepper. 5. To serve: Place the burgers on the lettuce, buns, or naan and top with the sauce.

Air Fried Beef Satay with Peanut Dipping Sauce

Prep time: 30 minutes | Cook time: 5 to 7 minutes | Serves 4

- 230 g bavette or skirt steak, sliced into 8 strips
- 2 teaspoons curry powder
- ½ teaspoon coarse or flaky salt
- Cooking spray
- Peanut Dipping sauce:
- 2 tablespoons creamy peanut butter
- 1 tablespoon reduced-salt soy sauce
- 2 teaspoons rice vinegar
- 1 teaspoon honey
- 1 teaspoon grated ginger

Special Equipment:
- 4 bamboo skewers, cut into halves and soaked in water for 20 minutes to keep them from burning while cooking

1. Preheat the air fryer to 180ºC. Spritz the air fryer basket with cooking spray. 2. In a bowl, place the steak strips and sprinkle with the curry powder and coarse or flaky salt to season. Thread the strips onto the soaked skewers. 3. Arrange the skewers in the prepared air fryer basket and spritz with cooking spray. Air fry for 5 to 7 minutes, or until the beef is well browned, turning halfway through. 4. In the meantime, stir together the peanut butter, soy sauce, rice vinegar, honey, and ginger in a bowl to make the dipping sauce. 5. Transfer the beef to the serving dishes and let rest for 5 minutes. Serve with the peanut dipping sauce on the side.

Spinach and Beef Braciole

Prep time: 25 minutes | Cook time: 1 hour 32 minutes | Serves 4

- ½ onion, finely chopped
- 1 teaspoon olive oil
- 80 ml red wine
- 475 g crushed tomatoes
- 1 teaspoon Italian seasoning
- ½ teaspoon garlic powder
- ¼ teaspoon crushed red pepper flakes
- 2 tablespoons chopped fresh parsley
- 2 bavette or skirt steaks (about 680 g)
- salt and freshly ground black pepper
- 475 g fresh spinach, chopped
- 1 clove minced garlic
- 120 g roasted red peppers, julienned
- 120 g grated pecorino cheese
- 60 g pine nuts, toasted and roughly chopped
- 2 tablespoons olive oil

1. Preheat the air fryer to 200ºC. 2. Toss the onions and olive oil together in a baking tray or casserole dish. Air fry at 200ºC for 5 minutes, stirring a couple times during the cooking process. Add the red wine, crushed tomatoes, Italian seasoning, garlic powder, red pepper flakes and parsley and stir. Cover the pan tightly with aluminium foil, lower the air fryer temperature to 180ºC and continue to air fry for 15 minutes. 3. While the sauce is simmering, prepare the beef. Using a meat mallet, pound the beef until it is ¼-inch thick. Season both sides of the beef with salt and pepper. Combine the spinach, garlic, red peppers, pecorino cheese, pine nuts and olive oil in a medium bowl. Season with salt and freshly ground black pepper. Disperse the mixture over the steaks. Starting at one of the short ends, roll the beef around the filling, tucking in the sides as you roll to ensure the filling is completely enclosed. Secure the beef rolls with toothpicks. 4. Remove the baking tray with the sauce from the air fryer and set it aside. Preheat the air fryer to 200ºC. 5. Brush or spray the beef rolls with a little olive oil and air fry at 200ºC for 12 minutes, rotating the beef during the cooking process for even browning. When the beef is browned, submerge the rolls into the sauce in the baking tray, cover the pan with foil and return it to the air fryer. Reduce the temperature of the air fryer to 120ºC and air fry for 60 minutes. 6. Remove the beef rolls from the sauce. Cut each roll into slices and serve, ladling some sauce overtop.

Chapter 6 Beef, Pork, and Lamb

Greek Stuffed Fillet

Prep time: 10 minutes | Cook time: 10 minutes | Serves 4

- 680 g venison or beef fillet, pounded to ¼ inch thick
- 3 teaspoons fine sea salt
- 1 teaspoon ground black pepper
- 60 g creamy goat cheese
- 120 g crumbled feta cheese (about 60 g)
- 60 g finely chopped onions
- 2 cloves garlic, minced

For Garnish/Serving (Optional):
- Yellow/American mustard
- Halved cherry tomatoes
- Extra-virgin olive oil
- Sprigs of fresh rosemary
- Lavender flowers

1. Spray the air fryer basket with avocado oil. Preheat the air fryer to 200ºC. 2. Season the fillet on all sides with the salt and pepper. 3. In a medium-sized mixing bowl, combine the goat cheese, feta, onions, and garlic. Place the mixture in the center of the tenderloin. Starting at the end closest to you, tightly roll the tenderloin like a jam roll. Tie the rolled tenderloin tightly with kitchen twine. 4. Place the meat in the air fryer basket and air fry for 5 minutes. Flip the meat over and cook for another 5 minutes, or until the internal temperature reaches 57ºC for medium-rare. 5. To serve, smear a line of yellow mustard on a platter, then place the meat next to it and add halved cherry tomatoes on the side, if desired. Drizzle with olive oil and garnish with rosemary sprigs and lavender flowers, if desired. 6. Best served fresh. Store leftovers in an airtight container in the fridge for 3 days. Reheat in a preheated 180ºC air fryer for 4 minutes, or until heated through.

Honey-Baked Pork Loin

Prep time: 30 minutes | Cook time: 22 to 25 minutes | Serves 6

- 60 ml honey
- 60 g freshly squeezed lemon juice
- 2 tablespoons soy sauce
- 1 teaspoon garlic powder
- 1 (900 g) pork loin
- 2 tablespoons vegetable oil

1. In a medium bowl, whisk together the honey, lemon juice, soy sauce, and garlic powder. Reserve half of the mixture for basting during cooking. 2. Cut 5 slits in the pork loin and transfer it to a resealable bag. Add the remaining honey mixture. Seal the bag and refrigerate to marinate for at least 2 hours. 3. Preheat the air fryer to 200ºC. Line the air fryer basket with parchment paper. 4. Remove the pork from the marinade, and place it on the parchment. Spritz with oil, then baste with the reserved marinade. 5. Cook for 15 minutes. Flip the pork, baste with more marinade and spritz with oil again. Cook for 7 to 10 minutes more until the internal temperature reaches 64ºC. Let rest for 5 minutes before serving.

BBQ Pork Steaks

Prep time: 5 minutes | Cook time: 15 minutes | Serves 4

- 4 pork steaks
- 1 tablespoon Cajun seasoning
- 2 tablespoons BBQ sauce
- 1 tablespoon vinegar
- 1 teaspoon soy sauce
- 96 g brown sugar
- 120 ml ketchup

1. Preheat the air fryer to 140ºC. 2. Sprinkle pork steaks with Cajun seasoning. 3. Combine remaining ingredients and brush onto steaks. 4. Add coated steaks to air fryer. Air fry 15 minutes until just browned. 5. Serve immediately.

Simple Beef Mince with Courgette

Prep time: 5 minutes | Cook time: 12 minutes | Serves 4

- 680 g beef mince
- 450 g chopped courgette
- 2 tablespoons extra-virgin olive oil
- 1 teaspoon dried oregano
- 1 teaspoon dried basil
- 1 teaspoon dried rosemary
- 2 tablespoons fresh chives, chopped

1. Preheat the air fryer to 200ºC. 2. In a large bowl, combine all the ingredients, except for the chives, until well blended. 3. Place the beef and courgette mixture in the baking tray. Air fry for 12 minutes, or until the beef is browned and the courgette is tender. 4. Divide the beef and courgette mixture among four serving dishes. Top with fresh chives and serve hot.

Parmesan-Crusted Pork Chops

Prep time: 5 minutes | Cook time: 12 minutes | Serves 4

- 1 large egg
- 120 g grated Parmesan cheese
- 4 (110 g) boneless pork chops
- ½ teaspoon salt
- ¼ teaspoon ground black pepper

1. Whisk egg in a medium bowl and place Parmesan in a separate medium bowl. 2. Sprinkle pork chops on both sides with salt and pepper. Dip each pork chop into egg, then press both sides into Parmesan. 3. Place pork chops into ungreased air fryer basket. Adjust the temperature to 200ºC and air fry for 12 minutes, turning chops halfway through cooking. Pork chops will be golden and have an internal temperature of at least 64ºC when done. Serve warm.

Banger and Peppers

Prep time: 7 minutes | Cook time: 35 minutes | Serves 4

- Oil, for spraying
- 900 g hot or sweet Italian-seasoned banger links, cut into thick slices
- 4 large peppers of any color, seeded and cut into slices
- 1 onion, thinly sliced
- 1 tablespoon olive oil
- 1 tablespoon chopped fresh parsley
- 1 teaspoon dried oregano
- 1 teaspoon dried basil
- 1 teaspoon balsamic vinegar

1. Line the air fryer basket with parchment and spray lightly with oil. 2. In a large bowl, combine the banger, peppers, and onion. 3. In a small bowl, whisk together the olive oil, parsley, oregano, basil, and balsamic vinegar. Pour the mixture over the banger and peppers and toss until evenly coated. 4. Using a slotted spoon, transfer the mixture to the prepared basket, taking care to drain out as much excess liquid as possible. 5. Air fry at 180°C for 20 minutes, stir, and cook for another 15 minutes, or until the banger is browned and the juices run clear.

Steaks with Walnut-Blue Cheese Butter

Prep time: 30 minutes | Cook time: 10 minutes | Serves 6

- 120 g unsalted butter, at room temperature
- 120 g crumbled blue cheese
- 2 tablespoons finely chopped walnuts
- 1 tablespoon minced fresh rosemary
- 1 teaspoon minced garlic
- ¼ teaspoon cayenne pepper
- Sea salt and freshly ground black pepper, to taste
- 680 g sirloin steaks, at room temperature

1. In a medium bowl, combine the butter, blue cheese, walnuts, rosemary, garlic, and cayenne pepper and salt and black pepper to taste. Use clean hands to ensure that everything is well combined. Place the mixture on a sheet of parchment paper and form it into a log. Wrap it tightly in cling film. Refrigerate for at least 2 hours or freeze for 30 minutes. 2. Season the steaks generously with salt and pepper. 3. Place the air fryer basket or grill pan in the air fryer. Set the air fryer to 200°C and let it preheat for 5 minutes. 4. Place the steaks in the basket in a single layer and air fry for 5 minutes. Flip the steaks, and cook for 5 minutes more, until an instant-read thermometer reads 49°C for medium-rare (or as desired). 5. Transfer the steaks to a plate. Cut the butter into pieces and place the desired amount on top of the steaks. Tent a piece of aluminium foil over the steaks and allow to sit for 10 minutes before serving. 6. Store any remaining butter in a sealed container in the refrigerator for up to 2 weeks.

Barbecue Ribs

Prep time: 5 minutes | Cook time: 30 minutes | Serves 4

- 1 (900 g) rack pork loin Back Ribs
- 1 teaspoon onion granules
- 1 teaspoon garlic powder
- 1 teaspoon light brown sugar
- 1 teaspoon dried oregano
- Salt and freshly ground black pepper, to taste
- Cooking oil spray
- 120 ml barbecue sauce

1. Use a sharp knife to remove the thin membrane from the back of the ribs. Cut the rack in half, or as needed, so the ribs fit in the air fryer basket. The best way to do this is to cut the ribs into 4- or 5-rib sections. 2. In a small bowl, stir together the onion granules, garlic powder, brown sugar, and oregano and season with salt and pepper. Rub the spice seasoning onto the front and back of the ribs. 3. Cover the ribs with cling film or foil and let sit at room temperature for 30 minutes. 4. Insert the crisper plate into the basket and the basket into the unit. Preheat the unit by selecting AIR ROAST, setting the temperature to 180°C, and setting the time to 3 minutes. Select START/STOP to begin. 5. Once the unit is preheated, spray the crisper plate with cooking oil. Place the ribs into the basket. It is okay to stack them. 6. Select AIR ROAST, set the temperature to 180°C, and set the time to 30 minutes. Select START/STOP to begin. 7. After 15 minutes, flip the ribs. Resume cooking for 15 minutes, or until a food thermometer registers 88°C. 8. When the cooking is complete, transfer the ribs to a serving dish. Drizzle the ribs with the barbecue sauce and serve.

Cinnamon-Beef Kofta

Prep time: 10 minutes | Cook time: 13 minutes per batch | Makes 12 koftas

- 680 g lean beef mince
- 1 teaspoon onion granules
- ¾ teaspoon ground cinnamon
- ¾ teaspoon ground dried turmeric
- 1 teaspoon ground cumin
- ¾ teaspoon salt
- ¼ teaspoon cayenne
- 12 (3½- to 4-inch-long) cinnamon sticks
- Cooking spray

1. Preheat the air fryer to 190°C. Spritz the air fryer basket with cooking spray. 2. Combine all the ingredients, except for the cinnamon sticks, in a large bowl. Toss to mix well. 3. Divide and shape the mixture into 12 balls, then wrap each ball around each cinnamon stick and leave a quarter of the length uncovered. 4. Arrange the beef-cinnamon sticks in the preheated air fryer and spritz with cooking spray. Work in batches to avoid overcrowding. 5. Air fry for 13 minutes or until the beef is browned. Flip the sticks halfway through. 6. Serve immediately.

Italian Lamb Chops with Avocado Mayo

Prep time: 5 minutes | Cook time: 12 minutes | Serves 2

- 2 lamp chops
- 2 teaspoons Italian herbs
- 2 avocados
- 120 ml mayonnaise
- 1 tablespoon lemon juice

1. Season the lamb chops with the Italian herbs, then set aside for 5 minutes. 2. Preheat the air fryer to 200ºC and place the rack inside. 3. Put the chops on the rack and air fry for 12 minutes. 4. In the meantime, halve the avocados and open to remove the pits. Spoon the flesh into a blender. 5. Add the mayonnaise and lemon juice and pulse until a smooth consistency is achieved. 6. Take care when removing the chops from the air fryer, then plate up and serve with the avocado mayo.

Bo Luc Lac

Prep time: 50 minutes | Cook time: 8 minutes | Serves 4

For the Meat:
- 2 teaspoons soy sauce
- 4 garlic cloves, minced
- 1 teaspoon coarse or flaky salt
- 2 teaspoons sugar
- ¼ teaspoon ground black pepper
- 1 teaspoon toasted sesame oil
- 680 g top rump steak, cut into 1-inch cubes
- Cooking spray

For the Salad:
- 1 head butterhead lettuce, leaves separated and torn into large pieces
- 60 g fresh mint leaves
- 120 g halved baby plum tomatoes
- ½ red onion, halved and thinly sliced
- 2 tablespoons apple cider vinegar
- 1 garlic clove, minced
- 2 teaspoons sugar
- ¼ teaspoon coarse or flaky salt
- ¼ teaspoon ground black pepper
- 2 tablespoons vegetable oil

For Serving:
- Lime wedges, for garnish
- Coarse salt and freshly cracked black pepper, to taste

1. Combine the ingredients for the meat, except for the steak, in a large bowl. Stir to mix well. 2. Dunk the steak cubes in the bowl and press to coat. Wrap the bowl in plastic and marinate under room temperature for at least 30 minutes. 3. Preheat the air fryer to 230ºC. Spritz the air fryer basket with cooking spray. 4. Discard the marinade and transfer the steak cubes in the preheated air fryer basket. You need to air fry in batches to avoid overcrowding. 5. Air fry for 4 minutes or until the steak cubes are lightly browned but still have a little pink. Shake the basket halfway through the cooking time. 6. Meanwhile, combine the ingredients for the salad in a separate large bowl. Toss to mix well. 7. Pour the salad in a large serving bowl and top with the steak cubes. Squeeze the lime wedges over and sprinkle with salt and black pepper before serving.

Rosemary Ribeye Steaks

Prep time: 10 minutes | Cook time: 15 minutes | Serves 2

- 60 g butter
- 1 clove garlic, minced
- Salt and ground black pepper, to taste
- 1½ tablespoons balsamic vinegar
- 60 g rosemary, chopped
- 2 ribeye steaks

1. Melt the butter in a frying pan over medium heat. Add the garlic and fry until fragrant. 2. Remove the frying pan from the heat and add the salt, pepper, and vinegar. Allow it to cool. 3. Add the rosemary, then pour the mixture into a Ziploc bag. 4. Put the ribeye steaks in the bag and shake well, coating the meat well. Refrigerate for an hour, then allow to sit for a further twenty minutes. 5. Preheat the air fryer to 200ºC. 6. Air fry the ribeye steaks for 15 minutes. 7. Take care when removing the steaks from the air fryer and plate up. 8. Serve immediately.

Lemon Pork with Marjoram

Prep time: 5 minutes | Cook time: 10 minutes | Serves 4

- 1 (450 g) pork tenderloin, cut into ½-inch-thick slices
- 1 tablespoon extra-virgin olive oil
- 1 tablespoon freshly squeezed lemon juice
- 1 tablespoon honey
- ½ teaspoon grated lemon zest
- ½ teaspoon dried marjoram leaves
- Pinch salt
- Freshly ground black pepper, to taste
- Cooking oil spray

1. Put the pork slices in a medium bowl. 2. In a small bowl, whisk the olive oil, lemon juice, honey, lemon zest, marjoram, salt, and pepper until combined. Pour this marinade over the tenderloin slices and gently massage with your hands to work it into the pork. 3. Insert the crisper plate into the basket and the basket into the unit. Preheat the unit by selecting AIR ROAST, setting the temperature to 200ºC, and setting the time to 3 minutes. Select START/STOP to begin. 4. Once the unit is preheated, spray the crisper plate with cooking oil. Place the pork into the basket. 5. Select AIR ROAST, set the temperature to 200ºC, and set the time to 10 minutes. Select START/STOP to begin. 6. When the cooking is complete, a food thermometer inserted into the pork should register at least 64ºC. Let the pork stand for 5 minutes and serve.

Southern Chilli

Prep time: 20 minutes | Cook time: 25 minutes | Serves 4

- 450 g beef mince (85% lean)
- 235 g minced onion
- 1 (794 g) tin tomato purée
- 1 (425 g) tin diced tomatoes
- 1 (425 g) tin red kidney beans, rinsed and drained
- 60 g Chili seasoning

1. Preheat the air fryer to 200ºC. 2. In a baking tray, mix the mince and onion. Place the pan in the air fryer. 3. Cook for 4 minutes. Stir and cook for 4 minutes more until browned. Remove the pan from the fryer. Drain the meat and transfer to a large bowl. 4. Reduce the air fryer temperature to 180ºC. 5. To the bowl with the meat, add in the tomato purée, diced tomatoes, kidney beans, and Chili seasoning. Mix well. Pour the mixture into the baking tray. 6. Cook for 25 minutes, stirring every 10 minutes, until thickened.

Beef and Pork Banger Meatloaf

Prep time: 20 minutes | Cook time: 25 minutes | Serves 4

- 340 g beef mince
- 110 g pork banger meat
- 235 g shallots, finely chopped
- 2 eggs, well beaten
- 3 tablespoons milk
- 1 tablespoon oyster sauce
- 1 teaspoon porcini mushrooms
- ½ teaspoon cumin powder
- 1 teaspoon garlic paste
- 1 tablespoon fresh parsley
- Salt and crushed red pepper flakes, to taste
- 235 g crushed cream crackers
- Cooking spray

1. Preheat the air fryer to 180ºC. Spritz a baking dish with cooking spray. 2. Mix all the ingredients in a large bowl, combining everything well. 3. Transfer to the baking dish and bake in the air fryer for 25 minutes. 4. Serve hot.

Marinated Steak Tips with Mushrooms

Prep time: 30 minutes | Cook time: 10 minutes | Serves 4

- 680 g rump steak, trimmed and cut into 1-inch pieces
- 230 g brown mushrooms, halved
- 60 ml Worcestershire sauce
- 1 tablespoon Dijon mustard
- 1 tablespoon olive oil
- 1 teaspoon paprika
- 1 teaspoon crushed red pepper flakes
- 2 tablespoons chopped fresh parsley (optional)

1. Place the beef and mushrooms in a gallon-size resealable bag. In a small bowl, whisk together the Worcestershire, mustard, olive oil, paprika, and red pepper flakes. Pour the marinade into the bag and massage gently to ensure the beef and mushrooms are evenly coated. Seal the bag and refrigerate for at least 4 hours, preferably overnight. Remove from the refrigerator 30 minutes before cooking. 2. Preheat the air fryer to 200ºC. 3. Drain and discard the marinade. Arrange the steak and mushrooms in the air fryer basket. Air fry for 10 minutes, pausing halfway through the baking time to shake the basket. Transfer to a serving plate and top with the parsley, if desired.

Ham Hock Mac and Cheese

Prep time: 20 minutes | Cook time: 25 minutes | Serves 4

- 2 large eggs, beaten
- 475 g cottage cheese, full-fat or low-fat
- 475 g grated sharp Cheddar cheese, divided
- 235 ml sour cream
- ½ teaspoon salt
- 1 teaspoon freshly ground black pepper
- 475 g uncooked elbow macaroni
- 2 gammon hocks (about 310 g each), meat removed and diced
- 1 to 2 tablespoons oil

1. In a large bowl, stir together the eggs, cottage cheese, 235 ml of the Cheddar cheese, sour cream, salt, and pepper. 2. Stir in the macaroni and the diced meat. 3. Preheat the air fryer to 180ºC. Spritz a baking tray with oil. 4. Pour the macaroni mixture into the prepared pan, making sure all noodles are covered with sauce. 5. Cook for 12 minutes. Stir in the remaining 235 ml of Cheddar cheese, making sure all the noodles are covered with sauce. Cook for 13 minutes more, until the noodles are tender. Let rest for 5 minutes before serving.

Mediterranean Beef Steaks

Prep time: 20 minutes | Cook time: 20 minutes | Serves 4

- 2 tablespoons soy sauce or tamari
- 3 heaping tablespoons fresh chives
- 2 tablespoons olive oil
- 3 tablespoons dry white wine
- 4 small-sized beef steaks
- 2 teaspoons smoked cayenne pepper
- ½ teaspoon dried basil
- ½ teaspoon dried rosemary
- 1 teaspoon freshly ground black pepper
- 1 teaspoon sea salt, or more to taste

1. Firstly, coat the steaks with the cayenne pepper, black pepper, salt, basil, and rosemary. 2. Drizzle the steaks with olive oil, white wine, and soy sauce. 3. Finally, roast in the air fryer for 20 minutes at 170ºC. Serve garnished with fresh chives. Bon appétit!

Chapter 6 Beef, Pork, and Lamb

Spinach and Mozzarella Steak Rolls

Prep time: 10 minutes | Cook time: 12 minutes | Makes 8 rolls

- 1 (450 g) bavette or skirt steak, butterflied
- 8 (30 g, ¼-inch-thick) slices low-moisture Mozzarella or other melting cheese
- 235 g fresh spinach leaves
- ½ teaspoon salt
- ¼ teaspoon ground black pepper

1. Place steak on a large plate. Place Mozzarella slices to cover steak, leaving 1-inch at the edges. Lay spinach leaves over cheese. Gently roll steak and tie with kitchen twine or secure with toothpicks. Carefully slice into eight pieces. Sprinkle each with salt and pepper. 2. Place rolls into ungreased air fryer basket, cut side up. Adjust the temperature to 200ºC and air fry for 12 minutes. Steak rolls will be browned and cheese will be melted when done and have an internal temperature of at least 64ºC for medium steak and 82ºC for well-done steak. Serve warm.

Mexican Pork Chops

Prep time: 5 minutes | Cook time: 15 minutes | Serves 2

- ¼ teaspoon dried oregano
- 1½ teaspoons taco seasoning or fajita seasoning mix
- 2 (110 g) boneless pork chops
- 2 tablespoons unsalted butter, divided

1. Preheat the air fryer to 200ºC. 2. Combine the dried oregano and taco seasoning in a small bowl and rub the mixture into the pork chops. Brush the chops with 1 tablespoon butter. 3. In the air fryer, air fry the chops for 15 minutes, turning them over halfway through to air fry on the other side. 4. When the chops are a brown color, check the internal temperature has reached 64ºC and remove from the air fryer. Serve with a garnish of remaining butter.

Jalapeño Popper Pork Chops

Prep time: 15 minutes | Cook time: 6 to 8 minutes | Serves 4

- 800 g bone-in, loin pork chops
- Sea salt and freshly ground black pepper, to taste
- 170 g cream cheese, at room temperature
- 110 g sliced bacon, cooked and crumbled
- 110 g Cheddar cheese, shredded
- 1 jalapeño, seeded and diced
- 1 teaspoon garlic powder

1. Cut a pocket into each pork chop, lengthwise along the side, making sure not to cut it all the way through. Season the outside of the chops with salt and pepper. 2. In a small bowl, combine the cream cheese, bacon, Cheddar cheese, jalapeño, and garlic powder. Divide this mixture among the pork chops, stuffing it into the pocket of each chop. 3. Set the air fryer to 200ºC. Place the pork chops in the air fryer basket in a single layer, working in batches if necessary. Air fry for 3 minutes. Flip the chops and cook for 3 to 5 minutes more, until an instant-read thermometer reads 64ºC. 4. Allow the chops to rest for 5 minutes, then serve warm.

Parmesan Herb Filet Mignon

Prep time: 20 minutes | Cook time: 13 minutes | Serves 4

- 450 g fillet mignon
- Sea salt and ground black pepper, to taste
- ½ teaspoon cayenne pepper
- 1 teaspoon dried basil
- 1 teaspoon dried rosemary
- 1 teaspoon dried thyme
- 1 tablespoon sesame oil
- 1 small-sized egg, well-whisked
- 120 g Parmesan cheese, grated

1. Season the fillet mignon with salt, black pepper, cayenne pepper, basil, rosemary, and thyme. Brush with sesame oil. 2. Put the egg in a shallow plate. Now, place the Parmesan cheese in another plate. 3. Coat the fillet mignon with the egg; then lay it into the Parmesan cheese. Set the air fryer to 180ºC. 4. Cook for 10 to 13 minutes or until golden. Serve with mixed salad leaves and enjoy!

Macadamia Nuts Crusted Pork Rack

Prep time: 5 minutes | Cook time: 35 minutes | Serves 2

- 1 clove garlic, minced
- 2 tablespoons olive oil
- 450 g rack of pork
- 235 g chopped macadamia nuts
- 1 tablespoon breadcrumbs
- 1 tablespoon rosemary, chopped
- 1 egg
- Salt and ground black pepper, to taste

1. Preheat the air fryer to 180ºC. 2. Combine the garlic and olive oil in a small bowl. Stir to mix well. 3. On a clean work surface, rub the pork rack with the garlic oil and sprinkle with salt and black pepper on both sides. 4. Combine the macadamia nuts, breadcrumbs, and rosemary in a shallow dish. Whisk the egg in a large bowl. 5. Dredge the pork in the egg, then roll the pork over the macadamia nut mixture to coat well. Shake the excess off. 6. Arrange the pork in the preheated air fryer and air fry for 30 minutes on both sides. Increase to 200ºC and fry for 5 more minutes or until the pork is well browned. 7. Serve immediately.

Cajun Bacon Pork Loin Fillet

Prep time: 30 minutes | Cook time: 20 minutes | Serves 6

- 680 g pork loin fillet or pork tenderloin
- 3 tablespoons olive oil
- 2 tablespoons Cajun spice mix
- Salt, to taste
- 6 slices bacon
- Olive oil spray

1. Cut the pork in half so that it will fit in the air fryer basket. 2. Place both pieces of meat in a resealable plastic bag. Add the oil, Cajun seasoning, and salt to taste, if using. Seal the bag and massage to coat all of the meat with the oil and seasonings. Marinate in the refrigerator for at least 1 hour or up to 24 hours. 3. Remove the pork from the bag and wrap 3 bacon slices around each piece. Spray the air fryer basket with olive oil spray. Place the meat in the air fryer. Set the air fryer to 180ºC for 15 minutes. Increase the temperature to 200ºC for 5 minutes. Use a meat thermometer to ensure the meat has reached an internal temperature of 64ºC. 4. Let the meat rest for 10 minutes. Slice into 6 medallions and serve.

Chapter 7

Fish and Seafood

Chapter 7 Fish and Seafood

Smoky Prawns and Chorizo Tapas

Prep time: 15 minutes | Cook time: 10 minutes | Serves 2 to 4

- 110 g Spanish (cured) chorizo, halved horizontally and sliced crosswise
- 230 g raw medium prawns, peeled and deveined
- 1 tablespoon extra-virgin olive oil
- 1 small shallot, halved and thinly sliced
- 1 garlic clove, minced
- 1 tablespoon finely chopped fresh oregano
- ½ teaspoon smoked Spanish paprika
- ¼ teaspoon kosher or coarse sea salt
- ¼ teaspoon black pepper
- 3 tablespoons fresh orange juice
- 1 tablespoon minced fresh parsley

1. Place the chorizo in a baking pan. Set the pan in the air fryer basket. Set the air fryer to 190°C for 5 minutes, or until the chorizo has started to brown and render its fat. 2. Meanwhile, in a large bowl, combine the prawns, olive oil, shallot, garlic, oregano, paprika, salt, and pepper. Toss until the prawns are well coated. 3. Transfer the prawns to the pan with the chorizo. Stir to combine. Place the pan in the air fryer basket. Cook for 10 minutes, stirring halfway through the cooking time. 4. Transfer the prawns and chorizo to a serving dish. Drizzle with the orange juice and toss to combine. Sprinkle with the parsley.

Bang Bang Prawns

Prep time: 15 minutes | Cook time: 14 minutes | Serves 4

Sauce:
- 115 g mayonnaise
- 60 ml sweet chilli sauce
- 2 to 4 tablespoons Sriracha

Prawns:
- 455 g jumbo raw prawns (21 to 25 count), peeled and deveined
- 2 tablespoons cornflour or rice flour
- 1 teaspoon minced fresh ginger
- ½ teaspoon kosher or coarse sea salt
- Vegetable oil spray

1. For the sauce: In a large bowl, combine the mayonnaise, chilli sauce, Sriracha, and ginger. Stir until well combined. Remove half of the sauce to serve as a dipping sauce. 2. For the prawns: Place the prawns in a medium bowl. Sprinkle the cornflour and salt over the prawns and toss until well coated. 3. Place the prawns in the air fryer basket in a single layer. (If they won't fit in a single layer, set a rack or trivet on top of the bottom layer of prawns and place the rest of the prawns on the rack.) Spray generously with vegetable oil spray. Set the air fryer to 180°C for 10 minutes, turning and spraying with additional oil spray halfway through the cooking time. 4. Remove the prawns and toss in the bowl with half of the sauce. Place the prawns back in the air fryer basket. Cook for an additional 4 to 5 minutes, or until the sauce has formed a glaze. 5. Serve the hot prawns with the reserved sauce for dipping.

Sea Bass with Potato Scales

Prep time: 10 minutes | Cook time: 10 minutes | Serves 2

- 2 fillets of sea bass, 170- to 230 g each
- Salt and freshly ground black pepper, to taste
- 60 ml mayonnaise
- 2 teaspoons finely chopped lemon zest
- 1 teaspoon chopped fresh thyme
- 2 Fingerling, or new potatoes, very thinly sliced into rounds
- Olive oil
- ½ clove garlic, crushed into a paste
- 1 tablespoon capers, drained and rinsed
- 1 tablespoon olive oil
- 1 teaspoon lemon juice, to taste

1. Preheat the air fryer to 200°C. 2. Season the fish well with salt and freshly ground black pepper. Mix the mayonnaise, lemon zest and thyme together in a small bowl. Spread a thin layer of the mayonnaise mixture on both fillets. Start layering rows of potato slices onto the fish fillets to simulate the fish scales. The second row should overlap the first row slightly. Dabbing a little more mayonnaise along the upper edge of the row of potatoes where the next row overlaps will help the potato slices stick. Press the potatoes onto the fish to secure them well and season again with salt. Brush or spray the potato layer with olive oil. 3. Transfer the fish to the air fryer and air fry for 8 to 10 minutes, depending on the thickness of your fillets. 1-inch of fish should take 10 minutes at 200°C. 4. While the fish is cooking, add the garlic, capers, olive oil and lemon juice to the remaining mayonnaise mixture to make the caper aïoli. 5. Serve the fish warm with a dollop of the aïoli on top or on the side.

Simple Buttery Cod

Prep time: 5 minutes | Cook time: 8 minutes | Serves 2

- 2 cod fillets, 110 g each
- 2 tablespoons salted butter, melted
- 1 teaspoon Old Bay seasoning
- ½ medium lemon, sliced

1. Place cod fillets into a round baking dish. Brush each fillet with butter and sprinkle with Old Bay seasoning. Lay two lemon slices on each fillet. Cover the dish with foil and place into the air fryer basket. 2. Adjust the temperature to 180°C and bake for 8 minutes. Flip halfway through the cooking time. When cooked, internal temperature should be at least 64°C. Serve warm.

Sole Fillets

Prep time: 10 minutes | Cook time: 5 to 8 minutes | Serves 4

- 1 egg white
- 1 tablespoon water
- 30 g panko breadcrumbs
- 2 tablespoons extra-light virgin olive oil
- 4 sole fillets, 110 g each
- Salt and pepper, to taste
- Olive or vegetable oil for misting or cooking spray

1. Preheat the air fryer to 390ºF (200ºC). 2. Beat together egg white and water in shallow dish. 3. In another shallow dish, mix panko crumbs and oil until well combined and crumbly (best done by hand). 4. Season sole fillets with salt and pepper to taste. Dip each fillet into egg mixture and then roll in panko crumbs, pressing in crumbs so that fish is nicely coated. 5. Spray the air fryer basket with nonstick cooking spray and add fillets. Air fry at 200ºC for 3 minutes. 6. Spray fish fillets but do not turn. Cook 2 to 5 minutes longer or until golden brown and crispy. Using a spatula, carefully remove fish from basket and serve.

Tuna Nuggets in Hoisin Sauce

Prep time: 15 minutes | Cook time: 5 to 7 minutes | Serves 4

- 120 ml hoisin sauce
- 2 tablespoons rice wine vinegar
- 2 teaspoons sesame oil
- 1 teaspoon garlic powder
- 2 teaspoons dried lemongrass
- ¼ teaspoon red pepper flakes
- ½ small onion, quartered and thinly sliced
- 230 g fresh tuna, cut into 1-inch cubes
- Cooking spray
- 560 g cooked jasmine rice

1. Mix the hoisin sauce, vinegar, sesame oil, and seasonings together. 2. Stir in the onions and tuna nuggets. 3. Spray a baking pan with nonstick spray and pour in tuna mixture. 4. Roast at 200ºC for 3 minutes. Stir gently. 5. Cook 2 minutes and stir again, checking for doneness. Tuna should be barely cooked through, just beginning to flake and still very moist. If necessary, continue cooking and stirring in 1-minute intervals until done. 6. Serve warm over hot jasmine rice.

Tuna Steak

Prep time: 10 minutes | Cook time: 12 minutes | Serves 4

- 455 g tuna steaks, boneless and cubed
- 1 tablespoon mustard
- 1 tablespoon avocado oil
- 1 tablespoon apple cider vinegar

1. Mix avocado oil with mustard and apple cider vinegar. 2. Then brush tuna steaks with mustard mixture and put in the air fryer basket. 3. Cook the fish at 180ºC for 6 minutes per side.

Oregano Tilapia Fingers

Prep time: 15 minutes | Cook time: 9 minutes | Serves 4

- 455 g tilapia fillet
- 30 g coconut flour
- 2 eggs, beaten
- ½ teaspoon ground paprika
- 1 teaspoon dried oregano
- 1 teaspoon avocado oil

1. Cut the tilapia fillets into fingers and sprinkle with ground paprika and dried oregano. 2. Then dip the tilapia fingers in eggs and coat in the coconut flour. 3. Sprinkle fish fingers with avocado oil and cook in the air fryer at 190ºC for 9 minutes.

Seasoned Tuna Steaks

Prep time: 5 minutes | Cook time: 9 minutes | Serves 4

- 1 teaspoon garlic powder
- ½ teaspoon salt
- ¼ teaspoon dried thyme
- ¼ teaspoon dried oregano
- 4 tuna steaks
- 2 tablespoons olive oil
- 1 lemon, quartered

1. Preheat the air fryer to 190ºC. 2. In a small bowl, whisk together the garlic powder, salt, thyme, and oregano. 3. Coat the tuna steaks with olive oil. Season both sides of each steak with the seasoning blend. Place the steaks in a single layer in the air fryer basket. 4. Roast for 5 minutes, then flip and roast for an additional 3 to 4 minutes.

Crab-Stuffed Avocado Boats

Prep time: 5 minutes | Cook time: 7 minutes | Serves 4

- 2 medium avocados, halved and pitted
- 230 g cooked crab meat
- ¼ teaspoon Old Bay seasoning
- 2 tablespoons peeled and diced brown onion
- 2 tablespoons mayonnaise

1. Scoop out avocado flesh in each avocado half, leaving ½ inch around edges to form a shell. Chop scooped-out avocado. 2. In a medium bowl, combine crab meat, Old Bay seasoning, onion, mayonnaise, and chopped avocado. Place ¼ mixture into each avocado shell. 3. Place avocado boats into ungreased air fryer basket. Adjust the temperature to 180°C and air fry for 7 minutes. Avocado will be browned on the top and mixture will be bubbling when done. Serve warm.

Golden Prawns

Prep time: 20 minutes | Cook time: 7 minutes | Serves 4

- 2 egg whites
- 30 g coconut flour
- 120 g Parmigiano-Reggiano, grated
- ½ teaspoon celery seeds
- ½ teaspoon porcini powder
- ½ teaspoon onion powder
- 1 teaspoon garlic powder
- ½ teaspoon dried rosemary
- ½ teaspoon sea salt
- ½ teaspoon ground black pepper
- 680 g prawns, peeled and deveined

1. Whisk the egg with coconut flour and Parmigiano-Reggiano. Add in seasonings and mix to combine well. 2. Dip your prawns in the batter. Roll until they are covered on all sides. 3. Cook in the preheated air fryer at 200°C for 5 to 7 minutes or until golden brown. Work in batches. Serve with lemon wedges if desired.

Parmesan Lobster Tails

Prep time: 5 minutes | Cook time: 7 minutes | Serves 4

- 4 (110 g) lobster tails
- 2 tablespoons salted butter, melted
- 1½ teaspoons Cajun seasoning, divided
- ¼ teaspoon salt
- ¼ teaspoon ground black pepper
- 40 g grated Parmesan cheese
- 15 g pork scratchings, finely crushed

1. Cut lobster tails open carefully with a pair of scissors and gently pull meat away from shells, resting meat on top of shells. 2. Brush lobster meat with butter and sprinkle with 1 teaspoon Cajun seasoning, ¼ teaspoon per tail. 3. In a small bowl, mix remaining Cajun seasoning, salt and pepper, Parmesan, and pork scratchings. Gently press ¼ mixture onto meat on each lobster tail. 4. Carefully place tails into ungreased air fryer basket. Adjust the temperature to 200°C and air fry for 7 minutes. Lobster tails will be crispy and golden on top and have an internal temperature of at least 64°C when done. Serve warm.

Fried Prawns

Prep time: 15 minutes | Cook time: 5 minutes | Serves 4

- 35 g self-raising flour
- 1 teaspoon paprika
- 1 teaspoon salt
- ½ teaspoon freshly ground black pepper
- 1 large egg, beaten
- 60 g finely crushed panko bread crumbs
- 20 frozen large prawns (about 900 g), peeled and deveined
- Cooking spray

1. In a shallow bowl, whisk the flour, paprika, salt, and pepper until blended. Add the beaten egg to a second shallow bowl and the bread crumbs to a third. 2. One at a time, dip the prawns into the flour, the egg, and the bread crumbs, coating thoroughly. 3. Preheat the air fryer to 200°C. Line the air fryer basket with baking paper. 4. Place the prawns on the baking paper and spritz with oil. 5. Air fry for 2 minutes. Shake the basket, spritz the prawns with oil, and air fry for 3 minutes more until lightly browned and crispy. Serve hot.

Southern-Style Catfish

Prep time: 10 minutes | Cook time: 12 minutes | Serves 4

- 4 (200 g) catfish fillets
- 80 ml heavy whipping cream
- 1 tablespoon lemon juice
- 55 g blanched finely ground almond flour
- 2 teaspoons Old Bay seasoning
- ½ teaspoon salt
- ¼ teaspoon ground black pepper

1. Place catfish fillets into a large bowl with cream and pour in lemon juice. Stir to coat. 2. In a separate large bowl, mix flour and Old Bay seasoning. 3. Remove each fillet and gently shake off excess cream. Sprinkle with salt and pepper. Press each fillet gently into flour mixture on both sides to coat. 4. Place fillets into ungreased air fryer basket. Adjust the temperature to 200°C and air fry for 12 minutes, turning fillets halfway through cooking. Catfish will be golden brown and have an internal temperature of at least 64°C when done. Serve warm.

Crab Legs

Prep time: 5 minutes | Cook time: 15 minutes | Serves 4

- 60 g salted butter, melted and divided
- 1.4 kg crab legs
- ¼ teaspoon garlic powder
- Juice of ½ medium lemon

1. In a large bowl, drizzle 2 tablespoons butter over crab legs. Place crab legs into the air fryer basket. 2. Adjust the temperature to 200ºC and air fry for 15 minutes. 3. Shake the air fryer basket to toss the crab legs halfway through the cooking time. 4. In a small bowl, mix remaining butter, garlic powder, and lemon juice. 5. To serve, crack open crab legs and remove meat. Dip in lemon butter.

Almond Pesto Salmon

Prep time: 5 minutes | Cook time: 12 minutes | Serves 2

- 60 g pesto
- 20 g sliced almonds, roughly chopped
- 2 (1½-inch-thick) salmon fillets (about 110 g each)
- 2 tablespoons unsalted butter, melted

1. In a small bowl, mix pesto and almonds. Set aside. 2. Place fillets into a round baking dish. 3. Brush each fillet with butter and place half of the pesto mixture on the top of each fillet. Place dish into the air fryer basket. 4. Adjust the temperature to 200ºC and set the timer for 12 minutes. 5. Salmon will easily flake when fully cooked and reach an internal temperature of at least 64ºC. Serve warm.

Cod with Avocado

Prep time: 30 minutes | Cook time: 10 minutes | Serves 2

- 90 g shredded cabbage
- 60 ml full-fat sour cream
- 2 tablespoons full-fat mayonnaise
- 20 g chopped pickled jalapeños
- 2 (85 g) cod fillets
- 1 teaspoon chilli powder
- 1 teaspoon cumin
- ½ teaspoon paprika
- ¼ teaspoon garlic powder
- 1 medium avocado, peeled, pitted, and sliced
- ½ medium lime

1. In a large bowl, place cabbage, sour cream, mayonnaise, and jalapeños. Mix until fully coated. Let sit for 20 minutes in the refrigerator. 2. Sprinkle cod fillets with chilli powder, cumin, paprika, and garlic powder. Place each fillet into the air fryer basket. 3. Adjust the temperature to 190ºC and set the timer for 10 minutes. 4. Flip the fillets halfway through the cooking time. When fully cooked, fish should have an internal temperature of at least 64ºC. 5. To serve, divide slaw mixture into two serving bowls, break cod fillets into pieces and spread over the bowls, and top with avocado. Squeeze lime juice over each bowl. Serve immediately.

Snapper with Shallot and Tomato

Prep time: 20 minutes | Cook time: 15 minutes | Serves 2

- 2 snapper fillets
- 1 shallot, peeled and sliced
- 2 garlic cloves, halved
- 1 pepper, sliced
- 1 small-sized serrano pepper, sliced
- 1 tomato, sliced
- 1 tablespoon olive oil
- ¼ teaspoon freshly ground black pepper
- ½ teaspoon paprika
- Sea salt, to taste
- 2 bay leaves

1. Place two baking paper sheets on a working surface. Place the fish in the center of one side of the baking paper. 2. Top with the shallot, garlic, peppers, and tomato. Drizzle olive oil over the fish and vegetables. Season with black pepper, paprika, and salt. Add the bay leaves. 3. Fold over the other half of the baking paper. Now, fold the paper around the edges tightly and create a half moon shape, sealing the fish inside. 4. Cook in the preheated air fryer at 200ºC for 15 minutes. Serve warm.

Parmesan-Crusted Halibut Fillets

Prep time: 5 minutes | Cook time: 10 minutes | Serves 4

- 2 medium-sized halibut fillets
- Dash of tabasco sauce
- 1 teaspoon curry powder
- ½ teaspoon ground coriander
- ½ teaspoon hot paprika
- Kosher or coarse sea salt, and freshly cracked mixed peppercorns, to taste
- 2 eggs
- 1½ tablespoons olive oil
- 75 g grated Parmesan cheese

1. Preheat the air fryer to 190ºC. 2. On a clean work surface, drizzle the halibut fillets with the tabasco sauce. Sprinkle with the curry powder, coriander, hot paprika, salt, and cracked mixed peppercorns. Set aside. 3. In a shallow bowl, beat the eggs until frothy. In another shallow bowl, combine the olive oil and Parmesan cheese. 4. One at a time, dredge the halibut fillets in the beaten eggs, shaking off any excess, then roll them over the Parmesan cheese until evenly coated. 5. Arrange the halibut fillets in the air fryer basket in a single layer and air fry for 10 minutes, or until the fish is golden brown and crisp. 6. Cool for 5 minutes before serving.

Catfish Bites

Prep time: 15 minutes | Cook time: 20 minutes | Serves 4

- Olive or vegetable oil, for spraying
- 455 g catfish fillets, cut into 2-inch pieces
- 235 ml buttermilk
- 35 g cornmeal
- 20 g plain flour
- 2 teaspoons Creole seasoning
- 120 ml yellow mustard

1. Line the air fryer basket with baking paper and spray lightly with oil. 2. Place the catfish pieces and buttermilk in a zip-top plastic bag, seal, and refrigerate for about 10 minutes. 3. In a shallow bowl, mix together the cornmeal, flour, and Creole seasoning. 4. Remove the catfish from the bag and pat dry with a paper towel. 5. Spread the mustard on all sides of the catfish, then dip them in the cornmeal mixture until evenly coated. 6. Place the catfish in the prepared basket. You may need to work in batches, depending on the size of your air fryer. Spray lightly with oil. 7. Air fry at 200ºC for 10 minutes, flip carefully, spray with oil, and cook for another 10 minutes. Serve immediately.

Foil-Packet Lobster Tail

Prep time: 15 minutes | Cook time: 12 minutes | Serves 2

- 2 lobster tails, 170 g each halved
- 2 tablespoons salted butter, melted
- ½ teaspoon Old Bay seasoning
- Juice of ½ medium lemon
- 1 teaspoon dried parsley

1. Place the two halved tails on a sheet of aluminium foil. Drizzle with butter, Old Bay seasoning, and lemon juice. 2. Seal the foil packets, completely covering tails. Place into the air fryer basket. 3. Adjust the temperature to 190ºC and air fry for 12 minutes. 4. Once done, sprinkle with dried parsley and serve immediately.

Blackened Fish

Prep time: 15 minutes | Cook time: 8 minutes | Serves 4

- 1 large egg, beaten
- Blackened seasoning, as needed
- 2 tablespoons light brown sugar
- 4 tilapia fillets, 110g each
- Cooking spray

1. In a shallow bowl, place the beaten egg. In a second shallow bowl, stir together the Blackened seasoning and the brown sugar. 2. One at a time, dip the fish fillets in the egg, then the brown sugar mixture, coating thoroughly. 3. Preheat the air fryer to 150ºC. Line the air fryer basket with baking paper. 4. Place the coated fish on the baking paper and spritz with oil. 5. Bake for 4 minutes. Flip the fish, spritz it with oil, and bake for 4 to 6 minutes more until the fish is white inside and flakes easily with a fork. 6. Serve immediately.

Baked Grouper with Tomatoes and Garlic

Prep time: 5 minutes | Cook time: 12 minutes | Serves 4

- 4 grouper fillets
- ½ teaspoon salt
- 3 garlic cloves, minced
- 1 tomato, sliced
- 45 g sliced Kalamata olives
- 10 g fresh dill, roughly chopped
- Juice of 1 lemon
- ¼ cup olive oil

1. Preheat the air fryer to 190ºC. 2. Season the grouper fillets on all sides with salt, then place into the air fryer basket and top with the minced garlic, tomato slices, olives, and fresh dill. 3. Drizzle the lemon juice and olive oil over the top of the grouper, then bake for 10 to 12 minutes, or until the internal temperature reaches 64ºC.

Fish Cakes

Prep time: 30 minutes | Cook time: 10 to 12 minutes | Serves 4

- 1 large russet potato, mashed
- 340 g cod or other white fish
- Salt and pepper, to taste
- Olive or vegetable oil for misting or cooking spray
- 1 large egg
- 50 g potato starch
- 30 g panko breadcrumbs
- 1 tablespoon fresh chopped chives
- 2 tablespoons minced onion

1. Peel potatoes, cut into cubes, and cook on stovetop till soft. 2. Salt and pepper raw fish to taste. Mist with oil or cooking spray, and air fry at 180ºC for 6 to 8 minutes, until fish flakes easily. If fish is crowded, rearrange halfway through cooking to ensure all pieces cook evenly. 3. Transfer fish to a plate and break apart to cool. 4. Beat egg in a shallow dish. 5. Place potato starch in another shallow dish, and panko crumbs in a third dish. 6. When potatoes are done, drain in colander and rinse with cold water. 7. In a large bowl, mash the potatoes and stir in the chives and onion. Add salt and pepper to taste, then stir in the fish. 8. If needed, stir in a tablespoon of the beaten egg to help bind the mixture. 9. Shape into 8 small, fat patties. Dust lightly with potato starch, dip in egg, and roll in panko crumbs. Spray both sides with oil or cooking spray. 10. Air fry for 10 to 12 minutes, until golden brown and crispy.

Salmon with Provolone Cheese

Prep time: 5 minutes | Cook time: 15 minutes | Serves 4

- 455 g salmon fillet, chopped
- 60 g Provolone or Edam, grated
- 1 teaspoon avocado oil
- ¼ teaspoon ground paprika

1. Sprinkle the salmon fillets with avocado oil and put in the air fryer. 2. Then sprinkle the fish with ground paprika and top with Provolone cheese. 3. Cook the fish at 180°C for 15 minutes.

Fish Fillets with Lemon-Dill Sauce

Prep time: 5 minutes | Cook time: 7 minutes | Serves 4

- 455 g snapper, grouper, or salmon fillets
- Sea salt and freshly ground black pepper, to taste
- 1 tablespoon avocado oil
- 60 g sour cream
- 60 g mayonnaise
- 2 tablespoons fresh dill, chopped, plus more for garnish
- 1 tablespoon freshly squeezed lemon juice
- ½ teaspoon grated lemon zest

1. Pat the fish dry with paper towels and season well with salt and pepper. Brush with the avocado oil. 2. Set the air fryer to 200°C. Place the fillets in the air fryer basket and air fry for 1 minute. 3. Lower the air fryer temperature to 160°C and continue cooking for 5 minutes. Flip the fish and cook for 1 minute more or until an instant-read thermometer reads 64°C. (If using salmon, cook it to 52°C /125°F for medium-rare.) 4. While the fish is cooking, make the sauce by combining the sour cream, mayonnaise, dill, lemon juice, and lemon zest in a medium bowl. Season with salt and pepper and stir until combined. Refrigerate until ready to serve. 5. Serve the fish with the sauce, garnished with the remaining dill.

Roasted Salmon Fillets

Prep time: 5 minutes | Cook time: 10 minutes | Serves 2

- 2 (230 g) skin-on salmon fillets, 1½ inches thick
- 1 teaspoon vegetable oil
- Salt and pepper, to taste
- Vegetable oil spray

1. Preheat the air fryer to 200°C. 2. Make foil sling for air fryer basket by folding 1 long sheet of aluminium foil so it is 4 inches wide. Lay sheet of foil widthwise across basket, pressing foil into and up sides of basket. Fold excess foil as needed so that edges of foil are flush with top of basket. Lightly spray foil and basket with vegetable oil spray. 3. Pat salmon dry with paper towels, rub with oil, and season with salt and pepper. Arrange fillets skin side down on sling in prepared basket, spaced evenly apart. Air fry salmon until center is still translucent when checked with the tip of a paring knife and registers 52°C (for medium-rare), 10 to 14 minutes, using sling to rotate fillets halfway through cooking. 4. Using the sling, carefully remove salmon from air fryer. Slide fish spatula along underside of fillets and transfer to individual serving plates, leaving skin behind. Serve.

Asian Marinated Salmon

Prep time: 30 minutes | Cook time: 6 minutes | Serves 2

Marinade:
- 60 ml wheat-free tamari or coconut aminos
- 2 tablespoons lime or lemon juice
- 2 tablespoons sesame oil
- 2 tablespoons powdered sweetener
- 2 teaspoons grated fresh ginger
- 2 cloves garlic, minced
- ½ teaspoon ground black pepper
- 2 (110 g) salmon fillets (about 1¼ inches thick)
- Sliced spring onions, for garnish

Sauce (Optional):
- 60 ml beef stock
- 60 ml wheat-free tamari
- 3 tablespoons powdered sweetener
- 1 tablespoon tomato sauce
- ⅛ teaspoon guar gum or xanthan gum (optional, for thickening)

1. Make the marinade: In a medium-sized shallow dish, stir together all the ingredients for the marinade until well combined. Place the salmon in the marinade. Cover and refrigerate for at least 2 hours or overnight. 2. Preheat the air fryer to 200°C. 3. Remove the salmon fillets from the marinade and place them in the air fryer, leaving space between them. Air fry for 6 minutes, or until the salmon is cooked through and flakes easily with a fork. 4. While the salmon cooks, make the sauce, if using: Place all the sauce ingredients except the guar gum in a medium-sized bowl and stir until well combined. Taste and adjust the sweetness to your liking. While whisking slowly, add the guar gum. Allow the sauce to thicken for 3 to 5 minutes. (The sauce tin be made up to 3 days ahead and stored in an airtight container in the fridge.) Drizzle the sauce over the salmon before serving. 5. Garnish the salmon with sliced spring onions before serving. Store leftovers in an airtight container in the fridge for up to 3 days. Reheat in a preheated 180°C air fryer for 3 minutes, or until heated through.

Coconut Prawns with Pineapple-Lemon Sauce

Prep time: 10 minutes | Cook time: 18 minutes | Serves 4

- 60 g light brown sugar
- 2 teaspoons cornflour
- ⅛ teaspoon plus ½ teaspoon salt, divided
- 110 g crushed pineapple with syrup
- 2 tablespoons freshly squeezed lemon juice
- 1 tablespoon yellow mustard
- 680 g raw large prawns, peeled and deveined
- 2 eggs
- 30 g plain flour
- 95 g desiccated, unsweetened coconut
- ¼ teaspoon garlic granules
- Olive oil spray

1. In a medium saucepan over medium heat, combine the brown sugar, cornflour, and ⅛ teaspoon of salt. 2. As the brown sugar mixture melts into a sauce, stir in the crushed pineapple with syrup, lemon juice, and mustard. Cook for about 4 minutes until the mixture thickens and begins to boil. Boil for 1 minute. Remove the pan from the heat, set aside, and let cool while you make the prawns. 3. Put the prawns on a plate and pat them dry with paper towels. 4. In a small bowl, whisk the eggs. 5. In a medium bowl, stir together the flour, desiccated coconut, remaining ½ teaspoon of salt, and garlic granules. 6. Insert the crisper plate into the basket and the basket into the unit. Preheat the unit to 200°C. 7. Dip the prawns into the egg and into the coconut mixture to coat. 8. Once the unit is preheated, place a baking paper liner into the basket. Place the coated prawns on the liner in a single layer and spray them with olive oil. 9. After 6 minutes, remove the basket, flip the prawns, and spray them with more olive oil. Reinsert the basket to resume cooking. Check the prawns after 3 minutes more. If browned, they are done; if not, resume cooking. 10. When the cooking is complete, serve with the prepared pineapple sauce.

Blackened Red Snapper

Prep time: 13 minutes | Cook time: 8 to 10 minutes | Serves 4

- 1½ teaspoons black pepper
- ¼ teaspoon thyme
- ¼ teaspoon garlic powder
- ⅛ teaspoon cayenne pepper
- 1 teaspoon olive oil
- 4 red snapper fillet portions, skin on, 110 g each
- 4 thin slices lemon
- Cooking spray

1. Mix the spices and oil together to make a paste. Rub into both sides of the fish. 2. Spray the air fryer basket with nonstick cooking spray and lay snapper steaks in basket, skin-side down. 3. Place a lemon slice on each piece of fish. 4. Roast at 200°C for 8 to 10 minutes. The fish will not flake when done, but it should be white through the center.

Chapter 8

Vegetables and Sides

Chapter 8 Vegetables and Sides

Gold Artichoke Hearts

Prep time: 15 minutes | Cook time: 8 minutes | Serves 4

- 12 whole artichoke hearts packed in water, drained
- 60 g plain flour
- 1 egg
- 40 g panko bread crumbs
- 1 teaspoon Italian seasoning
- Cooking oil spray

1. Squeeze any excess water from the artichoke hearts and place them on paper towels to dry. 2. Place the flour in a small bowl. 3. In another small bowl, beat the egg. 4. In a third small bowl, stir together the panko and Italian seasoning. 5. Dip the artichoke hearts in the flour, in the egg, and into the panko mixture until coated. 6. Insert the crisper plate into the basket and the basket into the unit. Preheat the unit by selecting AIR FRY, setting the temperature to 190°C, and setting the time to 3 minutes. Select START/STOP to begin. 7. Once the unit is preheated, spray the crisper plate and the basket with cooking oil. Place the breaded artichoke hearts into the basket, stacking them if needed. 8. Select AIR FRY, set the temperature to 190°C, and set the time to 8 minutes. Select START/STOP to begin. 9. After 4 minutes, use tongs to flip the artichoke hearts. I recommend flipping instead of shaking because the hearts are small, and this will help keep the breading intact. Re-insert the basket to resume cooking. 10. When the cooking is complete, the artichoke hearts should be deep golden brown and crisp. Cool for 5 minutes before serving.

Baked Jalapeño and Cheese Cauliflower Mash

Prep time: 10 minutes | Cook time: 15 minutes | Serves 6

- 1 (340 g) steamer bag cauliflower florets, cooked according to package instructions
- 2 tablespoons salted butter, softened
- 60 g cream cheese, softened
- 120 g shredded sharp Cheddar cheese
- 20 g pickled jalapeños
- ½ teaspoon salt
- ¼ teaspoon ground black pepper

1. Place cooked cauliflower into a food processor with remaining ingredients. Pulse twenty times until cauliflower is smooth and all ingredients are combined. 2. Spoon mash into an ungreased round nonstick baking dish. Place dish into air fryer basket. Adjust the temperature to 190°C and bake for 15 minutes. The top will be golden brown when done. Serve warm.

Tahini-Lemon Kale

Prep time: 5 minutes | Cook time: 15 minutes | Serves 2 to 4

- 60 g tahini
- 60 g fresh lemon juice
- 2 tablespoons olive oil
- 1 teaspoon sesame seeds
- ½ teaspoon garlic powder
- ¼ teaspoon cayenne pepper
- 110 g packed torn kale leaves (stems and ribs removed and leaves torn into palm-size pieces)
- coarse sea salt and freshly ground black pepper, to taste

1. In a large bowl, whisk together the tahini, lemon juice, olive oil, sesame seeds, garlic powder, and cayenne until smooth. Add the kale leaves, season with salt and black pepper, and toss in the dressing until completely coated. Transfer the kale leaves to a cake pan. 2. Place the pan in the air fryer and roast at 180°C, stirring every 5 minutes, until the kale is wilted and the top is lightly browned, about 15 minutes. Remove the pan from the air fryer and serve warm.

Cheddar Broccoli with Bacon

Prep time: 10 minutes | Cook time: 10 minutes | Serves 2

- 215 g fresh broccoli florets
- 1 tablespoon coconut oil
- 115 g shredded sharp Cheddar cheese
- 60 g full-fat sour cream
- 4 slices sugar-free bacon, cooked and crumbled
- 1 spring onion, sliced on the bias

1. Place broccoli into the air fryer basket and drizzle it with coconut oil. 2. Adjust the temperature to 180°C and set the timer for 10 minutes. 3. Toss the basket two or three times during cooking to avoid burned spots. 4. When broccoli begins to crisp at ends, remove from fryer. Top with shredded cheese, sour cream, and crumbled bacon and garnish with spring onion slices.

Broccoli with Sesame Dressing

Prep time: 5 minutes | Cook time: 10 minutes | Serves 4

- 425 g broccoli florets, cut into bite-size pieces
- 1 tablespoon olive oil
- ¼ teaspoon salt
- 2 tablespoons sesame seeds
- 2 tablespoons rice vinegar
- 2 tablespoons coconut aminos
- 2 tablespoons sesame oil
- ½ teaspoon xylitol
- ¼ teaspoon red pepper flakes (optional)

1. Preheat the air fryer to 200°C. 2. In a large bowl, toss the broccoli with the olive oil and salt until thoroughly coated. 3. Transfer the broccoli to the air fryer basket. Pausing halfway through the cooking time to shake the basket, air fry for 10 minutes until the stems are tender and the edges are beginning to crisp. 4. Meanwhile, in the same large bowl, whisk together the sesame seeds, vinegar, coconut aminos, sesame oil, xylitol, and red pepper flakes (if using). 5. Transfer the broccoli to the bowl and toss until thoroughly coated with the seasonings. Serve warm or at room temperature.

Fried Brussels Sprouts

Prep time: 10 minutes | Cook time: 18 minutes | Serves 4

- 1 teaspoon plus 1 tablespoon extra-virgin olive oil, divided
- 2 teaspoons minced garlic
- 2 tablespoons honey
- 1 tablespoon sugar
- 2 tablespoons freshly squeezed lemon juice
- 2 tablespoons rice vinegar
- 2 tablespoons sriracha
- 450 g Brussels sprouts, stems trimmed and any tough leaves removed, rinsed, halved lengthwise, and dried
- ½ teaspoon salt
- Cooking oil spray

1. In a small saucepan over low heat, combine 1 teaspoon of olive oil, the garlic, honey, sugar, lemon juice, vinegar, and sriracha. Cook for 2 to 3 minutes, or until slightly thickened. Remove the pan from the heat, cover, and set aside. 2. Place the Brussels sprouts in a resealable bag or small bowl. Add the remaining olive oil and the salt, and toss to coat. 3. Insert the crisper plate into the basket and the basket into the unit. Preheat the unit by selecting AIR FRY, setting the temperature to 200°C, and setting the time to 3 minutes. Select START/STOP to begin. 4. Once the unit is preheated, spray the crisper plate with cooking oil. Add the Brussels sprouts to the basket. 5. Select AIR FRY, set the temperature to 200°C, and set the time to 15 minutes. Select START/STOP to begin. 6. After 7 or 8 minutes, remove the basket and shake it to toss the sprouts. Reinsert the basket to resume cooking. 7. When the cooking is complete, the leaves should be crispy and light brown and the sprout centres tender. 8. Place the sprouts in a medium serving bowl and drizzle the sauce over the top. Toss to coat, and serve immediately.

Golden Pickles

Prep time: 10 minutes | Cook time: 15 minutes | Serves 4

- 14 dill pickles, sliced
- 30 g flour
- ⅛ teaspoon baking powder
- Pinch of salt
- 2 tablespoons cornflour plus
- 3 tablespoons water
- 6 tablespoons panko bread crumbs
- ½ teaspoon paprika
- Cooking spray

1. Preheat the air fryer to 200°C. 2. Drain any excess moisture out of the dill pickles on a paper towel. 3. In a bowl, combine the flour, baking powder and salt. 4. Throw in the cornflour and water mixture and combine well with a whisk. 5. Put the panko bread crumbs in a shallow dish along with the paprika. Mix thoroughly. 6. Dip the pickles in the flour batter, before coating in the bread crumbs. Spritz all the pickles with the cooking spray. 7. Transfer to the air fryer basket and air fry for 15 minutes, or until golden brown. 8. Serve immediately.

Asian-Inspired Roasted Broccoli

Prep time: 10 minutes | Cook time: 15 minutes | Serves 4

Broccoli:
- Oil, for spraying
- 450 g broccoli florets
- 2 teaspoons peanut oil
- 1 tablespoon minced garlic
- ½ teaspoon salt

Sauce:
- 2 tablespoons soy sauce
- 2 teaspoons honey
- 2 teaspoons Sriracha
- 1 teaspoon rice vinegar

Make the Broccoli 1. Line the air fryer basket with parchment and spray lightly with oil. 2. In a large bowl, toss together the broccoli, peanut oil, garlic, and salt until evenly coated. 3. Spread out the broccoli in an even layer in the prepared basket. 4. Air fry at 200°C for 15 minutes, stirring halfway through. Make the Sauce 5. Meanwhile, in a small microwave-safe bowl, combine the soy sauce, honey, Sriracha, and rice vinegar and microwave on high for about 15 seconds. Stir to combine. 6. Transfer the broccoli to a serving bowl and add the sauce. Gently toss until evenly coated and serve immediately.

Cheesy Loaded Broccoli

Prep time: 10 minutes | Cook time: 10 minutes | Serves 2

- 215 g fresh broccoli florets
- 1 tablespoon coconut oil
- ¼ teaspoon salt
- 120 g shredded sharp Cheddar cheese
- 60 g sour cream
- 4 slices cooked sugar-free bacon, crumbled
- 1 medium spring onion, trimmed and sliced on the bias

1. Place broccoli into ungreased air fryer basket, drizzle with coconut oil, and sprinkle with salt. Adjust the temperature to 180ºC and roast for 8 minutes. Shake basket three times during cooking to avoid burned spots. 2. Sprinkle broccoli with Cheddar and cook for 2 additional minutes. When done, cheese will be melted and broccoli will be tender. 3. Serve warm in a large serving dish, topped with sour cream, crumbled bacon, and spring onion slices.

Zesty Fried Asparagus

Prep time: 3 minutes | Cook time: 10 minutes | Serves 4

- Oil, for spraying
- 10 to 12 spears asparagus, trimmed
- 2 tablespoons olive oil
- 1 tablespoon garlic powder
- 1 teaspoon chilli powder
- ½ teaspoon ground cumin
- ¼ teaspoon salt

1. Line the air fryer basket with parchment and spray lightly with oil. 2. If the asparagus are too long to fit easily in the air fryer, cut them in half. 3. Place the asparagus, olive oil, garlic, chilli powder, cumin, and salt in a zip-top plastic bag, seal, and toss until evenly coated. 4. Place the asparagus in the prepared basket. 5. Roast at 200ºC for 5 minutes, flip, and cook for another 5 minutes, or until bright green and firm but tender.

Fried Courgette Salad

Prep time: 10 minutes | Cook time: 5 to 7 minutes | Serves 4

- 2 medium courgette, thinly sliced
- 5 tablespoons olive oil, divided
- 15 g chopped fresh parsley
- 2 tablespoons chopped fresh mint
- Zest and juice of ½ lemon
- 1 clove garlic, minced
- 65 g crumbled feta cheese
- Freshly ground black pepper, to taste

1. Preheat the air fryer to 200ºC. 2. In a large bowl, toss the courgette slices with 1 tablespoon of the olive oil. 3. Working in batches if necessary, arrange the courgette slices in an even layer in the air fryer basket. Pausing halfway through the cooking time to shake the basket, air fry for 5 to 7 minutes until soft and lightly browned on each side. 4. Meanwhile, in a small bowl, combine the remaining 4 tablespoons olive oil, parsley, mint, lemon zest, lemon juice, and garlic. 5. Arrange the courgette on a plate and drizzle with the dressing. Sprinkle the feta and black pepper on top. Serve warm or at room temperature.

Dijon Roast Cabbage

Prep time: 10 minutes | Cook time: 10 minutes | Serves 4

- 1 small head cabbage, cored and sliced into 1-inch-thick slices
- 2 tablespoons olive oil, divided
- ½ teaspoon salt
- 1 tablespoon Dijon mustard
- 1 teaspoon apple cider vinegar
- 1 teaspoon granular erythritol

1. Drizzle each cabbage slice with 1 tablespoon olive oil, then sprinkle with salt. Place slices into ungreased air fryer basket, working in batches if needed. Adjust the temperature to 180ºC and air fry for 10 minutes. Cabbage will be tender and edges will begin to brown when done. 2. In a small bowl, whisk remaining olive oil with mustard, vinegar, and erythritol. Drizzle over cabbage in a large serving dish. Serve warm.

Sweet-and-Sour Brussels Sprouts

Prep time: 10 minutes | Cook time: 20 minutes | Serves 2

- 70 g Thai sweet chilli sauce
- 2 tablespoons black vinegar or balsamic vinegar
- ½ teaspoon hot sauce, such as Tabasco
- 230 g Brussels sprouts, trimmed (large sprouts halved)
- 2 small shallots, cut into ¼-inch-thick slices
- coarse sea salt and freshly ground black pepper, to taste
- 2 teaspoons lightly packed fresh coriander leaves

1. In a large bowl, whisk together the chilli sauce, vinegar, and hot sauce. Add the Brussels sprouts and shallots, season with salt and pepper, and toss to combine. Scrape the Brussels sprouts and sauce into a cake pan. 2. Place the pan in the air fryer and roast at 190ºC, stirring every 5 minutes, until the Brussels sprouts are tender and the sauce is reduced to a sticky glaze, about 20 minutes. 3. Remove the pan from the air fryer and transfer the Brussels sprouts to plates. Sprinkle with the coriander and serve warm.

Stuffed Red Peppers with Herbed Ricotta and Tomatoes

Prep time: 10 minutes | Cook time: 20 minutes | Serves 4

- 2 red peppers
- 250 g cooked brown rice
- 2 plum tomatoes, diced
- 1 garlic clove, minced
- ¼ teaspoon salt
- ¼ teaspoon black pepper
- 115 g ricotta
- 3 tablespoons fresh basil, chopped
- 3 tablespoons fresh oregano, chopped
- 20 g shredded Parmesan, for topping

1. Preheat the air fryer to 180°C. 2. Cut the peppers in half and remove the seeds and stem. 3. In a medium bowl, combine the brown rice, tomatoes, garlic, salt, and pepper. 4. Distribute the rice filling evenly among the four pepper halves. 5. In a small bowl, combine the ricotta, basil, and oregano. Put the herbed cheese over the top of the rice mixture in each pepper. 6. Place the peppers into the air fryer and roast for 20 minutes. 7. Remove and serve with shredded Parmesan on top.

Caesar Whole Cauliflower

Prep time: 20 minutes | Cook time: 30 minutes | Serves 2 to 4

- 3 tablespoons olive oil
- 2 tablespoons red wine vinegar
- 2 tablespoons Worcestershire sauce
- 2 tablespoons grated Parmesan cheese
- 1 tablespoon Dijon mustard
- 4 garlic cloves, minced
- 4 oil-packed anchovy fillets, drained and finely minced
- coarse sea salt and freshly ground black pepper, to taste
- 1 small head cauliflower (about 450 g), green leaves trimmed and stem trimmed flush with the bottom of the head
- 1 tablespoon roughly chopped fresh flat-leaf parsley (optional)

1. In a liquid measuring jug, whisk together the olive oil, vinegar, Worcestershire, Parmesan, mustard, garlic, anchovies, and salt and pepper to taste. Place the cauliflower head upside down on a cutting board and use a paring knife to make an "x" through the full length of the core. Transfer the cauliflower head to a large bowl and pour half the dressing over it. Turn the cauliflower head to coat it in the dressing, then let it rest, stem-side up, in the dressing for at least 10 minutes and up to 30 minutes to allow the dressing to seep into all its nooks and crannies. 2. Transfer the cauliflower head, stem-side down, to the air fryer and air fry at 170°C or 25 minutes. Drizzle the remaining dressing over the cauliflower and air fry at 200°C until the top of the cauliflower is golden brown and the core is tender, about 5 minutes more. 3. Remove the basket from the air fryer and transfer the cauliflower to a large plate. Sprinkle with the parsley, if you like, and serve hot.

Maize and Coriander Salad

Prep time: 10 minutes | Cook time: 10 minutes | Serves 2

- 2 ears of maize, shucked (halved crosswise if too large to fit in your air fryer)
- 1 tablespoon unsalted butter, at room temperature
- 1 teaspoon chilli powder
- ¼ teaspoon garlic powder
- coarse sea salt and freshly ground black pepper, to taste
- 20 g lightly packed fresh coriander leaves
- 1 tablespoon sour cream
- 1 tablespoon mayonnaise
- 1 teaspoon adobo sauce (from a tin of chipotle peppers in adobo sauce)
- 2 tablespoons crumbled feta cheese
- Lime wedges, for serving

1. Brush the maize all over with the butter, then sprinkle with the chilli powder and garlic powder, and season with salt and pepper. Place the maize in the air fryer and air fry at 200°C, turning over halfway through, until the kernels are lightly charred and tender, about 10 minutes. 2. Transfer the ears to a cutting board, let stand 1 minute, then carefully cut the kernels off the cobs and move them to a bowl. Add the coriander leaves and toss to combine (the coriander leaves will wilt slightly). 3. In a small bowl, stir together the sour cream, mayonnaise, and adobo sauce. Divide the maize and coriander among plates and spoon the adobo dressing over the top. Sprinkle with the feta cheese and serve with lime wedges on the side.

Maple-Roasted Tomatoes

Prep time: 15 minutes | Cook time: 20 minutes | Serves 2

- 280 g cherry tomatoes, halved
- coarse sea salt, to taste
- 2 tablespoons maple syrup
- 1 tablespoon vegetable oil
- 2 sprigs fresh thyme, stems removed
- 1 garlic clove, minced
- Freshly ground black pepper

1. Place the tomatoes in a colander and sprinkle liberally with salt. Let stand for 10 minutes to drain. 2. Transfer the tomatoes cut-side up to a cake pan, then drizzle with the maple syrup, followed by the oil. Sprinkle with the thyme leaves and garlic and season with pepper. Place the pan in the air fryer and roast at 160°C until the tomatoes are soft, collapsed, and lightly caramelized on top, about 20 minutes. 3. Serve straight from the pan or transfer the tomatoes to a plate and drizzle with the juices from the pan to serve.

Garlic Roasted Broccoli

Prep time: 8 minutes | Cook time: 10 to 14 minutes | Serves 6

- 1 head broccoli, cut into bite-size florets
- 1 tablespoon avocado oil
- 2 teaspoons minced garlic
- ⅛ teaspoon red pepper flakes
- Sea salt and freshly ground black pepper, to taste
- 1 tablespoon freshly squeezed lemon juice
- ½ teaspoon lemon zest

1. In a large bowl, toss together the broccoli, avocado oil, garlic, red pepper flakes, salt, and pepper. 2. Set the air fryer to 190ºC. Arrange the broccoli in a single layer in the air fryer basket, working in batches if necessary. Roast for 10 to 14 minutes, until the broccoli is lightly charred. 3. Place the florets in a medium bowl and toss with the lemon juice and lemon zest. Serve.

Curried Fruit

Prep time: 10 minutes | Cook time: 20 minutes | Serves 6 to 8

- 210 g cubed fresh pineapple
- 200 g cubed fresh pear (firm, not overly ripe)
- 230 g frozen peaches, thawed
- 425 g tin dark, sweet, pitted cherries with juice
- 2 tablespoons brown sugar
- 1 teaspoon curry powder

1. Combine all ingredients in large bowl. Stir gently to mix in the sugar and curry. 2. Pour into a baking pan and bake at 180ºC for 10 minutes. 3. Stir fruit and cook 10 more minutes. 4. Serve hot.

Mashed Sweet Potato Tots

Prep time: 10 minutes | Cook time: 12 to 13 minutes per batch | Makes 18 to 24 tots

- 210 g cooked mashed sweet potatoes
- 1 egg white, beaten
- ⅛ teaspoon ground cinnamon
- 1 dash nutmeg
- 2 tablespoons chopped pecans
- 1½ teaspoons honey
- Salt, to taste
- 50 g panko bread crumbs
- Oil for misting or cooking spray

1. Preheat the air fryer to 200ºC. 2. In a large bowl, mix together the potatoes, egg white, cinnamon, nutmeg, pecans, honey, and salt to taste. 3. Place panko crumbs on a sheet of wax paper. 4. For each tot, use about 2 teaspoons of sweet potato mixture. To shape, drop the measure of potato mixture onto panko crumbs and push crumbs up and around potatoes to coat edges. Then turn tot over to coat other side with crumbs. 5. Mist tots with oil or cooking spray and place in air fryer basket in single layer. 6. Air fry at 200ºC for 12 to 13 minutes, until browned and crispy. 7. Repeat steps 5 and 6 to cook remaining tots.

Asian Tofu Salad

Prep time: 25 minutes | Cook time: 15 minutes | Serves 2

Tofu:
- 1 tablespoon soy sauce
- 1 tablespoon vegetable oil
- 1 teaspoon minced fresh ginger
- 1 teaspoon minced garlic
- 230 g extra-firm tofu, drained and cubed

Salad:
- 60 ml rice vinegar
- 1 tablespoon sugar
- 1 teaspoon salt
- 1 teaspoon black pepper
- 25 g sliced spring onions
- 120 g julienned cucumber
- 50 g julienned red onion
- 130 g julienned carrots
- 6 butter lettuce leaves

1. For the tofu: In a small bowl, whisk together the soy sauce, vegetable oil, ginger, and garlic. Add the tofu and mix gently. Let stand at room temperature for 10 minutes. 2. Arrange the tofu in a single layer in the air fryer basket. Set the air fryer to 200ºC for 15 minutes, shaking halfway through the cooking time. 3. Meanwhile, for the salad: In a large bowl, whisk together the vinegar, sugar, salt, pepper, and spring onions. Add the cucumber, onion, and carrots and toss to combine. Set aside to marinate while the tofu cooks. 4. To serve, arrange three lettuce leaves on each of two plates. Pile the marinated vegetables (and marinade) on the lettuce. Divide the tofu between the plates and serve.

Maize Croquettes

Prep time: 10 minutes | Cook time: 12 to 14 minutes | Serves 4

- 105 g leftover mashed potatoes
- 340 g maize kernels (if frozen, thawed, and well drained)
- ¼ teaspoon onion powder
- ⅛ teaspoon ground black pepper
- ¼ teaspoon salt
- 50 g panko bread crumbs
- Oil for misting or cooking spray

1. Place the potatoes and half the maize in food processor and pulse until maize is well chopped. 2. Transfer mixture to large bowl and stir in remaining maize, onion powder, pepper and salt. 3. Shape mixture into 16 balls. 4. Roll balls in panko crumbs, mist with oil or cooking spray, and place in air fryer basket. 5. Air fry at 180ºC for 12 to 14 minutes, until golden brown and crispy.

Garlic Cauliflower with Tahini

Prep time: 10 minutes | Cook time: 20 minutes | Serves 4

Cauliflower:
- 500 g cauliflower florets (about 1 large head)
- 6 garlic cloves, smashed and cut into thirds
- 3 tablespoons vegetable oil

Sauce:
- 2 tablespoons tahini (sesame paste)
- 2 tablespoons hot water
- 1 tablespoon fresh lemon juice
- ½ teaspoon ground cumin
- ½ teaspoon ground coriander
- ½ teaspoon coarse sea salt
- 1 teaspoon minced garlic
- ½ teaspoon coarse sea salt

1. For the cauliflower: In a large bowl, combine the cauliflower florets and garlic. Drizzle with the vegetable oil. Sprinkle with the cumin, coriander, and salt. Toss until well coated. 2. Place the cauliflower in the air fryer basket. Set the air fryer to 200°C for 20 minutes, turning the cauliflower halfway through the cooking time. 3. Meanwhile, for the sauce: In a small bowl, combine the tahini, water, lemon juice, garlic, and salt. (The sauce will appear curdled at first, but keep stirring until you have a thick, creamy, smooth mixture.) 4. Transfer the cauliflower to a large serving bowl. Pour the sauce over and toss gently to coat. Serve immediately.

Cauliflower with Lime Juice

Prep time: 10 minutes | Cook time: 7 minutes | Serves 4

- 215 g chopped cauliflower florets
- 2 tablespoons coconut oil, melted
- 2 teaspoons chilli powder
- ½ teaspoon garlic powder
- 1 medium lime
- 2 tablespoons chopped coriander

1. In a large bowl, toss cauliflower with coconut oil. Sprinkle with chilli powder and garlic powder. Place seasoned cauliflower into the air fryer basket. 2. Adjust the temperature to 180°C and set the timer for 7 minutes. 3. Cauliflower will be tender and begin to turn golden at the edges. Place into a serving bowl. 4. Cut the lime into quarters and squeeze juice over cauliflower. Garnish with coriander.

Chapter 9

Vegetarian Mains

Chapter 9 Vegetarian Mains

Caprese Aubergine Stacks

Prep time: 5 minutes | Cook time: 12 minutes | Serves 4

- 1 medium aubergine, cut into ¼-inch slices
- 2 large tomatoes, cut into ¼-inch slices
- 110 g fresh Mozzarella, cut into 14 g slices
- 2 tablespoons olive oil
- 60 g fresh basil, sliced

1. In a baking dish, place four slices of aubergine on the bottom. 2. Place a slice of tomato on top of each aubergine round, then Mozzarella, then aubergine. 3. Repeat as necessary. 4. Drizzle with olive oil. 5. Cover dish with foil and place dish into the air fryer basket. 6. Adjust the temperature to 180°C and bake for 12 minutes. 7. When done, aubergine will be tender. 8. Garnish with fresh basil to serve.

Broccoli-Cheese Fritters

Prep time: 5 minutes | Cook time: 20 to 25 minutes | Serves 4

- 235 g broccoli florets
- 235 g shredded Mozzarella cheese
- 180 g almond flour
- 120 g milled flaxseed, divided
- 2 teaspoons baking powder
- 1 teaspoon garlic powder
- Salt and freshly ground black pepper, to taste
- 2 eggs, lightly beaten
- 120 ml ranch dressing

1. Preheat the air fryer to 200°C. 2. In a food processor fitted with a metal blade, pulse the broccoli until very finely chopped. 3. Transfer the broccoli to a large bowl and add the Mozzarella, almond flour, 60 g milled flaxseed, baking powder, and garlic powder. 4. Stir until thoroughly combined. 5. Season to taste with salt and black pepper. 6. Add the eggs and stir again to form a sticky dough. 7. Shape the dough into 1¼-inch fritters. 8. Place the remaining 60 g milled flaxseed in a shallow bowl and roll the fritters in the meal to form an even coating. 9. Working in batches if necessary, arrange the fritters in a single layer in the basket of the air fryer and spray generously with olive oil. 10. Pausing halfway through the cooking time to shake the basket, air fry for 20 to 25 minutes until the fritters are golden brown and crispy. 11. Serve with the ranch dressing for dipping.

Baked Courgette

Prep time: 10 minutes | Cook time: 8 minutes | Serves 4

- 2 tablespoons salted butter
- 60 g diced white onion
- ½ teaspoon minced garlic
- 120 ml double cream
- 60 g full fat soft white cheese
- 235 g shredded extra mature Cheddar cheese
- 2 medium courgette, spiralized

1. In a large saucepan over medium heat, melt butter. 2. Add onion and sauté until it begins to soften, 1 to 3 minutes. 3. Add garlic and sauté for 30 seconds, then pour in cream and add soft white cheese. 4. Remove the pan from heat and stir in Cheddar. 5. Add the courgette and toss in the sauce, then put into a round baking dish. 6. Cover the dish with foil and place into the air fryer basket. 7. Adjust the temperature to 190°C and set the timer for 8 minutes. 8. After 6 minutes remove the foil and let the top brown for remaining cooking time. 9. Stir and serve.

Greek Stuffed Aubergine

Prep time: 15 minutes | Cook time: 20 minutes | Serves 2

- 1 large aubergine
- 2 tablespoons unsalted butter
- ¼ medium brown onion, diced
- 60 g chopped artichoke hearts
- 235 g fresh spinach
- 2 tablespoons diced red pepper
- 120 g crumbled feta

1. Slice aubergine in half lengthwise and scoop out flesh, leaving enough inside for shell to remain intact. 2. Take aubergine that was scooped out, chop it, and set aside. In a medium frying pan over medium heat, add butter and onion. 3. Sauté until onions begin to soften, about 3 to 5 minutes. Add chopped aubergine, artichokes, spinach, and pepper. 4. Continue cooking 5 minutes until peppers soften and spinach wilts. Remove from the heat and gently fold in the feta. 5. Place filling into each aubergine shell and place into the air fryer basket. 6. Adjust the temperature to 160°C and air fry for 20 minutes. 7. Aubergine will be tender when done. 8. Serve warm.

Stuffed Portobellos

Prep time: 10 minutes | Cook time: 8 minutes | Serves 4

- 85 g soft white cheese
- ½ medium courgette, trimmed and chopped
- 60 g seeded and chopped red pepper
- 350 g chopped fresh spinach leaves
- 4 large portobello mushrooms, stems removed
- 2 tablespoons coconut oil, melted
- ½ teaspoon salt

1. In a medium bowl, mix soft white cheese, courgette, pepper, and spinach. 2. Drizzle mushrooms with coconut oil and sprinkle with salt. 3. Scoop ¼ courgette mixture into each mushroom. 4. Place mushrooms into ungreased air fryer basket. 5. Adjust the temperature to 200ºC and air fry for 8 minutes. 6. Portobellos will be tender, and tops will be browned when done. 7. Serve warm.

Cheesy Cabbage Wedges

Prep time: 5 minutes | Cook time: 20 minutes | Serves 4

- 4 tablespoons melted butter
- 1 head cabbage, cut into wedges
- 235 g shredded Parmesan cheese
- Salt and black pepper, to taste
- 120 g shredded Mozzarella cheese

1. Preheat the air fryer to 190ºC. 2. Brush the melted butter over the cut sides of cabbage wedges and sprinkle both sides with the Parmesan cheese. 3. Season with salt and pepper to taste. 4. Place the cabbage wedges in the air fryer basket and air fry for 20 minutes, flipping the cabbage halfway through, or until the cabbage wedges are lightly browned. 5. Transfer the cabbage wedges to a plate and serve with the Mozzarella cheese sprinkled on top.

Potato and Broccoli with Tofu Scramble

Prep time: 15 minutes | Cook time: 30 minutes | Serves 3

- 600 g chopped red potato
- 2 tablespoons olive oil, divided
- 1 block tofu, chopped finely
- 2 tablespoons tamari
- 1 teaspoon turmeric powder
- ½ teaspoon onion powder
- ½ teaspoon garlic powder
- 120 g chopped onion
- 1 Kg broccoli florets

1. Preheat the air fryer to 200ºC. 2. Toss together the potatoes and 1 tablespoon of the olive oil. 3. Air fry the potatoes in a baking dish for 15 minutes, shaking once during the cooking time to ensure they fry evenly. 4. Combine the tofu, the remaining 1 tablespoon of the olive oil, turmeric, onion powder, tamari, and garlic powder together, stirring in the onions, followed by the broccoli. 5. Top the potatoes with the tofu mixture and air fry for an additional 15 minutes. 6. Serve warm.

Sweet Pepper Nachos

Prep time: 10 minutes | Cook time: 5 minutes | Serves 2

- 6 mini sweet peppers, seeded and sliced in half
- 180 g shredded Colby jack or Monterey Jack cheese
- 60 g sliced pickled jalapeños
- ½ medium avocado, peeled, pitted, and diced
- 2 tablespoons sour cream

1. Place peppers into an ungreased round non-stick baking dish. 2.Sprinkle with cheese and top with jalapeños. 3.Place dish into air fryer basket. 4.Adjust the temperature to 180°C and bake for 5 minutes. 5.Cheese will be melted and bubbly when done. 6.Remove dish from air fryer and top with avocado. 7.Drizzle with sour cream. 8.Serve warm.

Air Fryer Veggies with Halloumi

Prep time: 5 minutes | Cook time: 14 minutes | Serves 2

- 2 courgettes, cut into even chunks
- 1 large aubergine, peeled, cut into chunks
- 1 large carrot, cut into chunks
- 170 g halloumi cheese, cubed
- 2 teaspoons olive oil
- Salt and black pepper, to taste
- 1 teaspoon dried mixed herbs

1. Preheat the air fryer to 170°C. 2.Combine the courgettes, aubergine, carrot, cheese, olive oil, salt, and pepper in a large bowl and toss to coat well. 3.Spread the mixture evenly in the air fryer basket and air fry for 14 minutes until crispy and golden, shaking the basket once during cooking. 4.Serve topped with mixed herbs.

Mediterranean Pan Pizza

Prep time: 5 minutes | Cook time: 8 minutes | Serves 2

- 235 g shredded Mozzarella cheese
- ¼ medium red pepper, seeded and chopped
- 120 g chopped fresh spinach leaves
- 2 tablespoons chopped black olives
- 2 tablespoons crumbled feta cheese

1. Sprinkle Mozzarella into an ungreased round non-stick baking dish in an even layer. 2.Add remaining ingredients on top. 3.Place dish into air fryer basket. 4.Adjust the temperature to 180°C and bake for 8 minutes, checking halfway through to avoid burning. 5.Top of pizza will be golden brown, and the cheese melted when done. 6.Remove dish from fryer and let cool 5 minutes before slicing and serving.

Chapter 10

Desserts

Chapter 10 Desserts

Peach Fried Pies

Prep time: 15 minutes | Cook time: 20 minutes | Makes 8 pies

- 420 g tin sliced peaches in heavy syrup
- 1 teaspoon ground cinnamon
- 1 tablespoon cornflour
- 1 large egg
- All-purpose flour, for dusting
- Half a sheet of shortcrust pastry cut into 2

1. Reserving 2 tablespoons of syrup, drain the peaches well. Chop the peaches into bite-size pieces, transfer to a medium bowl, and stir in the cinnamon. 2. In a small bowl, stir together the reserved peach juice and cornflour until dissolved. Stir this slurry into the peaches. 3. In another small bowl, beat the egg. 4. Dust a cutting board or work surface with flour and spread the piecrusts on the prepared surface. Using a knife, cut each crust into 4 squares (8 squares total). 5. Place 2 tablespoons of peaches onto each dough square. Fold the dough in half and seal the edges. Using a pastry brush, spread the beaten egg on both sides of each hand pie. Using a knife, make 2 thin slits in the top of each pie. 6. Preheat the air fryer to 180ºC. 7. Line the air fryer basket with baking paper. Place 4 pies on the baking paper. 8. Cook for 10 minutes. Flip the pies, brush with beaten egg, and cook for 5 minutes more. Repeat with the remaining pies.

Protein Powder Doughnut Holes

Prep time: 25 minutes | Cook time: 6 minutes | Makes 12 holes

- 25g blanched finely ground almond flour
- 30 g low-carb vanilla protein powder
- 100 g granulated sweetener
- ½ teaspoon baking powder
- 1 large egg
- 5 tablespoons unsalted butter, melted
- ½ teaspoon vanilla extract

1. Mix all ingredients in a large bowl. Place into the freezer for 20 minutes. 2. Wet your hands with water and roll the dough into twelve balls. 3. Cut a piece of baking paper to fit your air fryer basket. Working in batches as necessary, place doughnut holes into the air fryer basket on top of baking paper. 4. Adjust the temperature to 190ºC and air fry for 6 minutes. 5. Flip doughnut holes halfway through the cooking time. 6. Let cool completely before serving.

Baked Brazilian Pineapple

Prep time: 10 minutes | Cook time: 10 minutes | Serves 4

- 60 g brown sugar
- 2 teaspoons ground cinnamon
- 1 small pineapple, peeled, cored, and cut into spears
- 3 tablespoons unsalted butter, melted

1. In a small bowl, mix the brown sugar and cinnamon until thoroughly combined. 2. Brush the pineapple spears with the melted butter. Sprinkle the cinnamon-sugar over the spears, pressing lightly to ensure it adheres well. 3. Place the spears in the air fryer basket in a single layer. (Depending on the size of your air fryer, you may have to do this in batches.) Set the air fryer to 200ºC and cook for 10 minutes for the first batch (6 to 8 minutes for the next batch, as the fryer will be preheated). Halfway through the cooking time, brush the spears with butter. 4. The pineapple spears are done when they are heated through, and the sugar is bubbling. Serve hot.

Shortcut Spiced Apple Butter

Prep time: 5 minutes | Cook time: 1 hour | Makes 1¼ cups

- Cooking spray
- 500 g store-bought unsweetened apple sauce
- 90 g packed light brown sugar
- 3 tablespoons fresh lemon juice
- ½ teaspoon kosher, or coarse sea salt
- ¼ teaspoon ground cinnamon
- ⅛ teaspoon ground allspice

1. Spray a cake pan with cooking spray. Whisk together all the ingredients in a bowl until smooth, then pour into the greased pan. Set the pan in the air fryer and bake at 170ºC until the apple mixture is caramelized, reduced to a thick purée, and fragrant, about 1 hour. 2. Remove the pan from the air fryer, stir to combine the caramelized bits at the edge with the rest, then let cool completely to thicken. Scrape the apple butter into a jar and store in the refrigerator for up to 2 weeks.

Cinnamon-Sugar Almonds

Prep time: 5 minutes | Cook time: 8 minutes | Serves 4

- 150 g whole almonds
- 2 tablespoons salted butter, melted
- 1 tablespoon granulated sugar
- ½ teaspoon ground cinnamon

1. In a medium bowl, combine the almonds, butter, sugar, and cinnamon. Mix well to ensure all the almonds are coated with the spiced butter. 2. Transfer the almonds to the air fryer basket and shake so they are in a single layer. Set the air fryer to 150°C, and cook for 8 minutes, stirring the almonds halfway through the cooking time. 3. Let cool completely before serving.

Pecan and Cherry Stuffed Apples

Prep time: 10 minutes | Cook time: 20 minutes | Serves 4

- 4 apples (about 565 g)
- 40 g chopped pecans
- 50 g dried tart cherries
- 1 tablespoon melted butter
- 3 tablespoons brown sugar
- ¼ teaspoon allspice
- Pinch salt
- Ice cream, for serving

1. Cut off top ½ inch from each apple; reserve tops. With a melon baller, core through stem ends without breaking through the bottom. (Do not trim bases.) 2. Preheat the air fryer to 180°C. Combine pecans, cherries, butter, brown sugar, allspice, and a pinch of salt. Stuff mixture into the hollow centers of the apples. Cover with apple tops. Put in the air fryer basket, using tongs. Air fry for 20 to 25 minutes, or just until tender. 3. Serve warm with ice cream.

Baked Apples and Walnuts

Prep time: 6 minutes | Cook time: 20 minutes | Serves 4

- 4 small Granny Smith apples
- 50 g chopped walnuts
- 40 g light brown sugar
- 2 tablespoons butter, melted
- 1 teaspoon ground cinnamon
- ½ teaspoon ground nutmeg
- 120 ml water, or apple juice

1. Cut off the top third of the apples. Spoon out the core and some of the flesh and discard. Place the apples in a small air fryer baking pan. 2. Insert the crisper plate into the basket and the basket into the unit. Preheat to 180°C. 3. In a small bowl, stir together the walnuts, brown sugar, melted butter, cinnamon, and nutmeg. Spoon this mixture into the centers of the hollowed-out apples. 4. Once the unit is preheated, pour the water into the crisper plate. Place the baking pan into the basket. 5. Bake for 20 minutes. 6. When the cooking is complete, the apples should be bubbly and fork tender.

Vanilla Scones

Prep time: 20 minutes | Cook time: 10 minutes | Serves 6

- 55 g coconut flour
- ½ teaspoon baking powder
- 1 teaspoon apple cider vinegar
- 2 teaspoons mascarpone
- 60 ml double cream
- 1 teaspoon vanilla extract
- 1 tablespoon granulated sweetener

1. In the mixing bowl, mix coconut flour with baking powder, apple cider vinegar, mascarpone, double cream, vanilla extract, and sweetener. 2. Knead the dough and cut into scones. 3. Then put them in the air fryer basket and sprinkle with cooking spray. 4. Cook the vanilla scones at 190°C for 10 minutes.

Cream-Filled Sponge Cakes

Prep time: 10 minutes | Cook time: 10 minutes | Makes 4 cakes

- Coconut, or avocado oil, for spraying
- 1 tube croissant dough
- 4 Swiss rolls
- 1 tablespoon icing sugar

1. Line the air fryer basket with baking paper, and spray lightly with oil. 2. Unroll the dough into a single flat layer and cut it into 4 equal pieces. 3. Place 1 sponge cake in the center of each piece of dough. Wrap the dough around the cake, pinching the ends to seal. 4. Place the wrapped cakes in the prepared basket, and spray lightly with oil. 5. Bake at 90°C for 5 minutes, flip, spray with oil, and cook for another 5 minutes, or until golden brown. 6. Dust with the icing sugar and serve.

Pumpkin Spice Pecans

Prep time: 5 minutes | Cook time: 6 minutes | Serves 4

- 125 g whole pecans
- 50 g granulated sweetener
- 1 large egg white
- ½ teaspoon ground cinnamon
- ½ teaspoon pumpkin pie spice
- ½ teaspoon vanilla extract

1. Toss all ingredients in a large bowl until pecans are coated. Place into the air fryer basket. 2. Adjust the temperature to 150°C and air fry for 6 minutes. 3. Toss two to three times during cooking. 4. Allow to cool completely. Store in an airtight container up to 3 days.

Appendix 1: Basic Kitchen Conversions & Equivalents

DRY MEASUREMENTS CONVERSION CHART

3 teaspoons = 1 tablespoon = 1/16 cup

6 teaspoons = 2 tablespoons = 1/8 cup

12 teaspoons = 4 tablespoons = 1/4 cup

24 teaspoons = 8 tablespoons = 1/2 cup

36 teaspoons = 12 tablespoons = 3/4 cup

48 teaspoons = 16 tablespoons = 1 cup

METRIC TO US COOKING CONVERSIONS

OVEN TEMPERATURES

120 °C = 250 °F

160 °C = 320 °F

180 °C = 350 °F

205 °C = 400 °F

220 °C = 425 °F

LIQUID MEASUREMENTS CONVERSION CHART

8 fluid ounces = 1 cup = 1/2 pint = 1/4 quart

16 fluid ounces = 2 cups = 1 pint = 1/2 quart

32 fluid ounces = 4 cups = 2 pints = 1 quart = 1/4 gallon

128 fluid ounces = 16 cups = 8 pints = 4 quarts = 1 gallon

BAKING IN GRAMS

1 cup flour = 140 grams

1 cup sugar = 150 grams

1 cup powdered sugar = 160 grams

1 cup heavy cream = 235 grams

VOLUME

1 milliliter = 1/5 tsp

5 ml = 1 tsp

15 ml = 1 tbsp

240 ml = 1 cup or 8 fluid ounces

1 liter = 34 fluid ounces

WEIGHT

1 gram = 0.035 ounces

100 grams = 3.5 ounces

500 grams = 1.1 pounds

1 kilogram = 35 ounces

Appendix 2: Recipes Index

A

Air Fried Beef Satay with Peanut Dipping Sauce	37
Air Fried Broccoli	18
Air Fried Shishito Peppers	17
Air Fryer Veggies with Halloumi	62
Almond Pesto Salmon	48
Apple Cider Doughnut Holes	10
Artichoke and Olive Pitta Flatbread	24
Asian Marinated Salmon	50
Asian Tofu Salad	57
Asian-Inspired Roasted Broccoli	54
Avocado and Egg Burrito	13

B

Bacon and Spinach Egg Muffins	4
Bacon Eggs on the Go	5
Bacon, Broccoli and Cheese Bread Pudding	4
Bacon-and-Eggs Avocado	5
Bacon-Wrapped A Pickled Gherkin Spear	22
Bacon-Wrapped Chicken Breasts Rolls	27
Bacon-Wrapped Hot Dogs	14
Baked Apples and Walnuts	65
Baked Brazilian Pineapple	64
Baked Courgette	60
Baked Grouper with Tomatoes and Garlic	49
Baked Halloumi with Greek Salsa	16
Baked Jalapeño and Cheese Cauliflower Mash	53
Baked Spanakopita Dip	22
Banana-Nut Muffins	5
Bang Bang Prawns	45
Banger and Peppers	39
Banger Stuffed Peppers	8
Barbecue Ribs	39
BBQ Pork Steaks	38
Beef and Pork Banger Meatloaf	41
Beef Bratwursts	18
Beef Jerky	13
Blackened Fish	49
Blackened Red Snapper	51
Bo Luc Lac	40
Breaded Turkey Cutlets	29
Breakfast Calzone	7
Breakfast Cobbler	9
Broccoli with Sesame Dressing	54
Broccoli-Cheese Fritters	60
Buffalo Chicken Cheese Sticks	30
Bunless Breakfast Turkey Burgers	5
Buttermilk Breaded Chicken	29
Buttermilk-Fried Drumsticks	33
Buttery Sweet Potatoes	18

C

Caesar Whole Cauliflower	56
Cajun Bacon Pork Loin Fillet	43
Caprese Aubergine Stacks	60
Carrot Chips	22
Catfish Bites	49
Cauliflower with Lime Juice	58
Cheddar Broccoli with Bacon	53
Cheddar-Ham-Corn Muffins	7
Cheese-Stuffed Blooming Onion	22
Cheesy Cabbage Wedges	61
Cheesy Loaded Broccoli	55
Chicken and Gammon Meatballs with Dijon Sauce	27
Chicken Legs with Leeks	32
Chicken Manchurian	31
Chicken Paillard	28
Chicken Patties	32
Chicken Pesto Parmigiana	29
Chinese-Inspired Spareribs	14
Chipotle Aioli Wings	28
Chipotle Drumsticks	29
Cinnamon Rolls	8
Cinnamon-Beef Kofta	39
Cinnamon-Sugar Almonds	65
Coconut Chicken Wings with Mango Sauce	30
Coconut Prawns with Pineapple-Lemon Sauce	51

Cod with Avocado	48
Cornish Hens with Honey-Lime Glaze	31
Crab Legs	48
Crab-Stuffed Avocado Boats	47
Cream-Filled Sponge Cakes	65
Crispy Breaded Beef Cubes	24
Crispy Chilli Chickpeas	23
Crispy Duck with Cherry Sauce	34
Crispy Green Tomato Slices	23
Crunchy Chicken Tenders	33
Crunchy Fried Okra	16
Curried Fruit	57

D

Dijon Roast Cabbage	55

E

Easy Cajun Chicken Drumsticks	34
Egg in a Hole	4
Egg Tarts	8
Everything Bagels	7

F

Fish and Vegetable Tacos	13
Fish Cakes	49
Fish Fillets with Lemon-Dill Sauce	50
Foil-Packet Lobster Tail	49
French Garlic Chicken	33
Fried Artichoke Hearts	23
Fried Brussels Sprouts	54
Fried Courgette Salad	55
Fried Dill Pickles with Buttermilk Dressing	24
Fried Prawns	47

G

Garlic Cauliflower with Tahini	58
Garlic Roasted Broccoli	57
Garlicky Knots with Parsley	5
Gold Artichoke Hearts	53
Golden Chicken Cutlets	28
Golden Pickles	54
Golden Prawns	47

Golden Salmon and Carrot Croquettes	20
Greek Chicken Souvlaki	27
Greek Stuffed Aubergine	60
Greek Stuffed Fillet	38

H

Ham Hock Mac and Cheese	41
Harissa-Rubbed Chicken	31
Hearty Cheddar Biscuits	6
Herb-Roasted Veggies	17
Homemade Cherry Breakfast Tarts	9
Honey-Apricot Muesli with Greek Yoghurt	6
Honey-Baked Pork Loin	38

I

Indian Fennel Chicken	28
Italian Lamb Chops with Avocado Mayo	40
Italian Rice Balls	21

J

Jalapeño Popper Pork Chops	42
Jalapeño Poppers	23

K

Kheema Burgers	37

L

Lemon Chicken with Garlic	30
Lemon Pork with Marjoram	40
Lemon-Blueberry Muffins	10
Lettuce-Wrapped Turkey and Mushroom Meatballs	32

M

Macadamia Nuts Crusted Pork Rack	42
Maize and Coriander Salad	56
Maize Croquettes	57
Maple Muesli	8
Maple-Roasted Tomatoes	56
Marinated Steak Tips with Mushrooms	41
Mashed Sweet Potato Tots	57

Mediterranean Beef Steaks	41
Mediterranean Pan Pizza	62
Mexican Pork Chops	42
Mushroom Tarts	21

N

Nacho Chicken Fries	32

O

Old Bay Tilapia	13
Oregano Tilapia Fingers	46

P

Parmesan Herb Filet Mignon	42
Parmesan Lobster Tails	47
Parmesan-Crusted Halibut Fillets	48
Parmesan-Crusted Pork Chops	38
Peach Fried Pies	64
Pecan and Cherry Stuffed Apples	65
Pecan Rolls	12
Pecan Turkey Cutlets	33
Personal Cauliflower Pizzas	12
Pickle Chips	23
Pork Chops with Caramelized Onions	36
Potato and Broccoli with Tofu Scramble	61
Prawns Egg Rolls	20
Protein Powder Doughnut Holes	64
Pumpkin Spice Pecans	65
Purple Potato Chips with Rosemary	16

R

Roasted Salmon Fillets	50
Rosemary Ribeye Steaks	40
Rosemary-Garlic Shoestring Fries	20

S

Salmon with Provolone Cheese	50
Scotch Eggs	7
Sea Bass with Potato Scales	45
Seasoned Tuna Steaks	46
Shishito Peppers with Herb Dressing	24
Shortcut Spiced Apple Butter	64
Simple Beef Mince with Courgette	38
Simple Buttery Cod	46
Simple Scotch Eggs	6
Smoky Chicken Leg Quarters	30
Smoky Prawns and Chorizo Tapas	45
Snapper with Shallot and Tomato	48
Soft white cheese Stuffed Jalapeño Chillies Poppers	25
Sole Fillets	46
Southern Chilli	41
Southern-Style Catfish	47
Southwest Corn and Pepper Roast	17
Spice-Coated Steaks with Cucumber and Snap Pea Salad	36
Spinach and Beef Braciole	37
Spinach and Mozzarella Steak Rolls	42
Spiralized Potato Nest with Tomato Tomato Ketchup	21
Steak Tips and Potatoes	13
Steaks with Walnut-Blue Cheese Butter	39
Strawberry Toast	4
Stuffed Portobellos	61
Stuffed Red Peppers with Herbed Ricotta and Tomatoes	56
Sweet and Spicy Turkey Meatballs	34
Sweet Pepper Nachos	62
Sweet-and-Sour Brussels Sprouts	55

T

Tahini-Lemon Kale	53
Teriyaki Rump Steak with Broccoli and Capsicum	36
Thai-Style Cornish Game Hens	31
Traditional Queso Fundido	18
Tuna Nuggets in Hoisin Sauce	46
Tuna Steak	46
Turkey Banger Breakfast Pizza	9

V

Vanilla Muesli	6
Vanilla Scones	65
Veggie Tuna Melts	12

Z

Zesty Fried Asparagus	55

Printed in Great Britain
by Amazon